Endangered and Threatened Wildlife of the Chesapeake Bay Region:
Delaware, Maryland, and Virginia

A Cooperative Project of
The Chesapeake Bay Foundation
and the U. S. Fish and Wildlife Service

Endangered and Threatened Wildlife of the Chesapeake Bay Region:
Delaware, Maryland, and Virginia

Christopher P. White

TIDEWATER PUBLISHERS
Centreville, Maryland

Copyright © 1982 by Tidewater Publishers

All rights reserved. No part of this book may be used or reproduced in any manner whatsoever without written permission except in the case of brief quotations embodied in critical articles and reviews. For information, address Tidewater Publishers, Centreville, Maryland 21617.

Library of Congress Cataloging in Publication Data

White, Christopher P., 1956-
    Endangered and threatened wildlife of the Chesapeake Bay Region.

    Bibliography: p.
    Includes index.
    1. Endangered species—Chesapeake Bay region (Md. and Va.) I. Title.
QL84.22.C43W44   333.95′416′097521   81-85605
ISBN 0-87033-287-2   AACR2

Manufactured in the United States of America
First edition

Contents

Foreword	VII
Preface	IX
Acknowledgments	XI
Introduction	3
Section I: Endangered and Threatened Wildlife in the Tri-State Region	
MAMMALS THREATENED WITH EXTINCTION	13
Gray myotis	16
Indiana myotis	18
Virginia big-eared bat	20
Delmarva Peninsula fox squirrel	22
INTRODUCTION TO THE WHALES	25
Sperm whale	26
Blue whale	28
Fin whale	30
Sei whale	32
Humpback whale	34
Black right whale	36
Eastern cougar	38
BIRDS THREATENED WITH EXTINCTION	40
Eastern brown pelican	42
Bald eagle	44
American peregrine falcon	46
Arctic peregrine falcon	48
Red-cockaded woodpecker	50
Bachman's warbler	52
Kirtland's warbler	54
REPTILES AND AMPHIBIANS THREATENED WITH EXTINCTION	56
INTRODUCTION TO THE SEA TURTLES	59
Green turtle	60
Hawksbill turtle	62
Loggerhead turtle	64
Kemp's ridley turtle	66
Leatherback turtle	68

CONTENTS

FISHES THREATENED WITH EXTINCTION	70
Shortnose sturgeon	72
Slender chub	74
Spotfin chub	76
Yellowfin madtom	78
Maryland darter	80
ARTHROPODS THREATENED WITH EXTINCTION	82
Madison Cave isopod	84
Hay's spring amphipod	86
MOLLUSCS THREATENED WITH EXTINCTION	88
Virginia fringed mountain snail	90
INTRODUCTION TO THE MUSSELS	93
Appalachian monkey-face pearly mussel	94
Cumberland monkey-face pearly mussel	96
Birdwing pearly mussel	98
Dromedary pearly mussel	100
Green-blossom pearly mussel	102
Tan riffle shell mussel	104
Fine-rayed pigtoe mussel	106
Shiny pigtoe mussel	108
PLANTS THREATENED WITH EXTINCTION	110
Small whorled pogonia	112
Virginia round-leaf birch	114

Section II: Vertebrates in Danger of Extirpation from the Tri-State Area

INTRODUCTION	116
MAMMALS	118
BIRDS	120
REPTILES	122
AMPHIBIANS	124
FISHES	126

Appendix

TABLE I: Endangered and Threatened Species in Delaware, Maryland, and Virginia	129
TABLE II: Rare or Declining Vertebrate Species in Danger of Extirpation in Delaware, Maryland, and Virginia	136
Glossary	140
Selected References	143
Index	144

Foreword

By the year 2000, up to a million species of plants and animals may have become extinct worldwide. This irreversible process is probably the least recognized and most far-reaching crisis of our time. Life forms that have evolved slowly over millions of years in complex and intricate relationships with other species are now being destroyed at a rate which is accelerating with alarming rapidity. One thousand species per year is a conservative estimate. By the end of this decade the figure could be as high as ten thousand per year, or one species per hour. We know that species of economic, life-sustaining, and esthetic value will be lost and that worldwide environmental stability will be threatened. We can only guess how disastrous this loss of biological diversity will be for man's future well-being. Professor E. O. Wilson of Harvard has said that the folly for which future generations will not forgive us will not be limited nuclear war or economic collapse (terrible as the results of these catastrophes might be, they could be repaired in a few generations) but rather the ongoing loss of genetic and species diversity which will take millions of years to correct.

The Chesapeake Bay region, subject of this timely book, is rich in plant and animal species. It contains the largest and most commercially productive estuary in the United States. It is also under tremendous stress from increasing human activity: farming, fishing, industry, and recreation. In this way, it is an important microcosm nationally and globally.

As a lifelong resident, I am well acquainted with the beauty and biological richness of this diverse area of marshes, swamps, deciduous forests, pine woods, dunes, and beaches. I have also observed with growing concern the decline of huge populations of waterfowl, such as the canvasback duck, and the effects of overfishing and pollution. The way in which we protect and manage the natural resources of the Chesapeake Bay region will not only directly affect present and future residents but could have more widespread consequences. Careful planning and successful solutions here can provide examples for conservation work elsewhere—not only in this country but around the world.

This book sounds an alert in describing the treasures of our biological heritage that we are in danger of losing. The next step is up to us.

Russell E. Train, President
World Wildlife Fund—U. S.

Preface

The threatened and endangered wildlife covered in this field guide are residents, migrants, or visitors in the states of Delaware, Maryland, and Virginia, and their coastal waters. The Chesapeake Bay watershed is the regional focus, but plants and animals within the Ohio River drainage of Maryland and Virginia are included as well.

The primary purpose of the book is to describe native flora and fauna in danger of extinction (i.e., species threatened with extermination throughout their entire ranges). A secondary section of the text reports on vertebrate animals possibly in danger of extirpation from the tri-state region but which are common or stable in other parts of their domains. Species lists for the two sections appear in the Appendix.

All common and specific names are the currently accepted vernacular of the American scientific community. Species and subspecies are listed in phylogenetic sequence within each major taxonomic group, although the groups themselves are in reverse sequence (e.g., mammals, birds, fishes, molluscs). Only native species and subspecies found within the region in the past 25 years are included; exotics are not addressed.

The federally protected species and subspecies appearing in this book are the "endangered" and "threatened" plants and animals designated by the federal government as of February 1982. This federal list is subject to additions and deletions as species and subspecies are reviewed.

Terms used to designate the population status of plants and animals are defined as follows:

Endangered

A species or subspecies which is in danger of extinction throughout all or a significant portion of its range. Includes only those plants and animals currently listed as "endangered" under the provisions of the Endangered Species Act of 1973.

Threatened

A species or subspecies which is likely to become "endangered" within the foreseeable future throughout all or a significant portion of its range. Includes only those plants and animals currently listed as "threatened" under the provisions of the Endangered Species Act of 1973.

Proposed Endangered or Threatened

A species or subspecies which has received federal attention by virtue of a "proposed rule-making" published in the *Federal Register,* proposing to list the plant or animal as "endangered" or "threatened."

Potentially Threatened

A species or subspecies whose prospects for survival are perhaps in danger, now or in the foreseeable future, throughout all or a significant portion of its range, but for which further study is needed to make this determination. Includes plants and animals currently "under review" by the U. S. Fish and Wildlife Service.

In Danger of Extirpation

A species or subspecies which may be common or stable elsewhere in its range but which is in danger of elimination from the states of Delaware, Maryland, and Virginia because of a potential or realized threat to the rare, peripheral, or disjunct population(s) in this region.

Status Undetermined

A species or subspecies for which there is insufficient data to determine accurately its status.

Acknowledgments

In an effort to educate the public about the plight of endangered and threatened wildlife and the endeavors to bring about their recovery, the Chesapeake Bay Foundation and the U. S. Fish and Wildlife Service (USFWS) sponsored the research necessary to complete this field guide. In particular, Martha Carlisle and Andy Moser of the Delmarva Area Office (USFWS) and Paul Nickerson of the Regional Office (USFWS) assisted in data gathering and editing the text. John D. Green, Area Manager, Delmarva Area Office (USFWS), and Dr. Paul Opler, Office of Endangered Species (USFWS), provided staff support in this cooperative effort.

A large number of scientists from various institutions shared their recent data, unpublished information, and opinions with the author. I thank the following for their timely correspondence and technical expertise: Ray E. Ashton, Jr., John E. Cooper, and Steven P. Platania, North Carolina State Museum of Natural History; Thomas E. Bowman and Charles O. Handley, Jr., National Museum of Natural History, Smithsonian Institution; John T. Brady, St. Louis District, U. S. Army Corps of Engineers; Mitchell A. Byrd, College of William and Mary; Joseph A. Chapman, George A. Feldhamer, and J. Edward Gates, Appalachian Environmental Laboratory, University of Maryland; Kenneth M. Chitwood, Atlanta Regional Office (USFWS); William S. Clark and Keith W. Cline, Raptor Information Center, National Wildlife Federation; Robert Currie, Asheville Area Office (USFWS); Richard Dyer and Roger Hogan, Boston Regional Office (USFWS); Charles M. Frisbie, Maryland Tidewater Administration; John D. Groves, Philadelphia Zoological Society; John R. Holsinger and Robert K. Rose, Old Dominion University; Sally R. Hopkins, South Carolina Wildlife and Marine Resources Department; Leslie Hubricht, Meridian, Mississippi; Jerome A. Jackson, Mississippi State University; Eugene R. McCaffrey, New York Department of Environmental Conservation; Richard Neves and Terry L. Sharik, Virginia Polytechnic Institute and State University; Arnold W. Norden, Natural History Society of Maryland; Warren Parker, Asheville Area Office

(USFWS); Peter C. H. Pritchard, Florida Audubon Society; Chandler S. Robbins, Patuxent Wildlife Research Center (USFWS); Frank J. Schwartz, Institute of Marine Sciences, University of North Carolina; Frederick R. Scott, Virginia Society of Ornithology; Alan Solem, Chicago Field Museum of Natural History; Salvatore A. Testaverde, National Marine Fisheries Service; Franklin J. Tobey, Jr., Purcellville, Virginia; Martin L. Wiley, Chesapeake Biological Laboratory, University of Maryland; Jim Williams, Steve Chambers, Kenneth Dodd, Mike Bentzien, Ronald Nowak, Jay Sheppard, and Tom Strekal, Office of Endangered Species (USFWS); and Lovett E. Williams, Jr., University of Florida.

At the state level, H. Lloyd Alexander, Jr., Delaware Division of Fish and Wildlife, Gary J. Taylor and Steve Dawson, Maryland Wildlife Administration, and John P. Randolph, Virginia Commission of Game and Inland Fisheries, furnished information and lent assistance to the project.

I am grateful to William C. Baker, Richard R. Gardner, Stuart W. Lehman, Lisa Simeone, and Mary Tod Winchester of the Chesapeake Bay Foundation for their encouragement and valued support.

C. P. W.

Annapolis, Maryland
February 1982

Endangered and Threatened Wildlife of the Chesapeake Bay Region:
Delaware, Maryland, and Virginia

Introduction

> The theory of natural selection is grounded on the belief that each new variety and ultimately each new species is produced and maintained by having some advantage over those with which it comes into competition; and the consequent extinction of the less-favoured forms almost inevitably follows.
>
> The old notion of all the inhabitants of the earth having been swept away by catastrophes at successive periods is very generally given up. . . . On the contrary, we have every reason to believe, from the study of the tertiary formations, that species and groups of species gradually disappear, one after another, first from one spot, then from another, and finally from the world. . . . [R]arity precedes extinction; and we know that this has been the progress of events with those animals which have been exterminated, either locally or wholly, through man's agency.
>
> Charles Darwin, *The Origin of Species,* 1872

In the 110 years since Darwin presented his theory of evolution through natural selection of favored, more adaptable species, population biologists have agreed with the corollary that extinction of less adapted forms is a natural process integral to the evolution of life. Just as populations are kept in check by the balance of births and deaths, the number of different species is determined by the rates of speciation and extinction. In the natural equilibrium of a stable environment these two rates are equal; and, in this scenario, species diversity is only limited by the variety of available habitats and life modes. The new replaces the old, but the diversity remains the same. Throughout prehistory, natural environmental changes led to extinctions of flying reptiles, land dinosaurs, trilobites, and the like. Their demise increased the opportunity for the success of new life forms during the course of geologic time.

THE DECLINE OF DIVERSITY

If extinction, the irreversible loss of a breeding group of individuals, is a natural phenomenon, one might ask why there is so much concern about endangered species today. Of what possible significance is the loss of the furbish lousewort, the snail darter, or the whooping crane, all recently threatened by the proposed construction of hydroelectric dams in Maine, Tennessee, and Wyoming, respectively? How is the future of mankind altered by the recent extinction of the Tecopa pupfish? Is life diminished by the passing of the great auk, the passenger pigeon, or the Carolina parakeet?

The significance of modern day extinctions lies in the fact that the overwhelming majority of these plants and animals have been exterminated as a direct result of man's actions. The normal process of extinction has been accelerated and distorted by the human practices of exploiting natural resources. Man has the ability to alter the environment and disrupt natural ecosystems more dramatically and at a faster rate than all natural forces taken together.

During a 3,000-year period towards the end of the Pleistocene, for example, when an unusually large number of animals perished, North American extinctions tallied about 50 mammals and 40 birds. The extinction rate was thus 3 species per 100 years. Although this was an exceptionally high number, it is dwarfed by the more than 120 species which have been exterminated during the past century in the continental United States alone. Because of man's intervention in the natural process of extinction, the parallel phenomenon of speciation cannot keep pace. As a consequence, the total number of unique species on earth is declining.

A Survey of Extinctions in North America

Since the arrival of European settlers at Jamestown in 1607, over 200 species of native flora and fauna have become extinct in the United States, exclusive of Hawaii. Additionally, hundreds of subspecies, including the eastern elk (*Cervus elaphus canadensis*) which roamed the Chesapeake Bay region, have declined to the point of extinction because of man's intervention.

Bird species have suffered the worst fate in recent times among all vertebrate animals on the Atlantic coast. The Labrador duck (*Camptorhynchus labradorius*) became extinct in 1875 primarily because of commercial hunting pressure. The last passenger pigeon (*Ectopistes migratorius*) died in captivity in 1914 after the population was drastically and irreversibly reduced by excessive killing and alteration of its habitat. Thirteen years earlier, the colorful Carolina parakeet (*Conuropis carolinensis*) suffered the same fate for identical reasons. The heath-hen (*Tympanuchus cupido cupido*) vanished forever in 1932.

Recent extinctions in the Chesapeake Bay region may also include two plants, Long's stargrass (*Hypoxis longii*), last collected in Virginia Beach in 1934, and water-hyssop (*Bacopa simulans*), most recently seen on the Chickahominy River, Virginia, in 1941. The clear-wing moth (*Synanthedon castaneae*), which exclusively fed on the American chestnut before the blight fungus caused the tree's decline, was last observed in Virginia near the Potomac River in 1914. The moth has not been sighted anywhere since it was collected in South Carolina in 1936. In 1893, the harelip sucker (*Lagochila lacera*), a piscine inhabitant of the Ohio River and its tributaries, became extinct. The last Virginia record of this fish was in 1888 from the North Fork Holston River, a river flowing westward into the Ohio River Basin.

Today a total of 236 plants and animals found in the United States are designated "endangered" by the U. S. Department of the Interior. Another 47 are considered "threatened" in all or a significant portion of their ranges. In the states of Delaware, Maryland, and Virginia, 39 species and subspecies are on the federal list as "endangered" or "threatened" and an additional 2 species occurring in the Chesapeake Bay watershed are currently proposed for federal listing. These species are in imminent danger and their survival depends on federal protection.

Causes for Species Extinctions

While overhunting was responsible for a large part of the man-induced extinctions in North America prior to 1900, the most prevalent cause of endangerment since then has been habitat alteration and destruction. Among the activities most damaging to native wildlife have been clear-cutting of forests, monocultural agriculture and forestry practices, overgrazing by domestic animals, strip mining, road construction, urbanization and pollution, wetlands drainage, stream channelization, and dam construction with associated valley-flooding upstream and flow and temperature alteration downstream.

The impact of habitat loss on the population size of a species is best understood in the context of the theory of island biogeography. This theory, developed by MacArthur and Wilson at Princeton and Harvard universities, respectively, in the 1960s, demonstrates a relationship between size of range and extinction. The central hypothesis is that the number of species inhabiting an "island" or isolated habitat (e.g., a mountain peak, a secluded marsh, or a lone stand of timber) is a function of the island's area and distance from the main population. The smaller the isolated habitat and the farther its distance from the main population, the fewer the number of species that can successfully colonize the "island." This theory demonstrates that each species has a minimum range for survival. A viable population of ivory-billed woodpeckers, for example, required at least 160 square kilometers of cypress swamp and bottomland forest. Larger animals of higher trophic levels, such as carnivores and birds of prey, have greater range requisites and are more susceptible to extinction from habitat restriction. For this reason, large carnivores are absent from islands such as Hawaii and the Galapagos Archipelago.

While the effects of habitat degradation from air, water, and noise pollution are often difficult to demonstrate, the consequences of direct habitat alteration are better understood. The clear-cutting of forest nearly devastated the Delmarva fox squirrel before a recovery plan was adopted. The destruction of beaches and dunes through shoreline development and the use of off-road vehicles have forced the roseate tern and other shorebirds to abandon former nesting sites. Along with overfishing, the construction of dams on the tributaries of the Chesapeake Bay has severely depleted the brood stocks of anadromous fishes such as the shortnose sturgeon (*Acipenser brevirostrum*) and the American shad (*Alosa sapidissima*). Other human activities can be just as detrimental. The widespread use of pesticides, for example, reduced the bald eagle (*Haliaeetus leucocephalus*) and peregrine falcon (*Falco peregrinus*) to the brink of extinction before the ban of DDT in 1972.

PRESERVING THE DIVERSITY OF LIFE

Biologically, the loss of a species or subspecies is equated to the loss of a unique gene pool which determines the appearance and characteristics of individuals within a population (e.g., the black throat patch of the male Bachman's warbler). The loss, no matter how small, lessens the diversity of life. It is this diversity that keeps each ecosystem in balance or equilibrium.

Because our scientific knowledge is still too limited to ascertain the immediate or long-term worth of a given plant or animal except for harvestable species, a monetary value cannot be placed on each endangered species. However, there are many examples to show that the preservation of a particular species has been of direct benefit to our daily lives. Specifically of what importance were penicillium molds before Fleming discovered penicillin in 1928? Before Edward Jenner invented vaccination, of what value was the cowpox virus? Did man understand the worth of rubber trees before Goodyear experimented with its sap? The endangered snow leopard has a unique chemistry which enabled researchers in veterinary science to develop the distemper vaccine for domestic cats. The armadillo has now become an important factor in the study of leprosy, the aloe plant has received widespread acceptance as a sunburn preventative and remedy, and a drug derived from the Madagascar periwinkle plant is now being used to treat leukemia. These are but a few which could be cited since the list of beneficial uses for wildlife is quite extensive. Over 40 percent of medicinal drugs are derived from living plants and animals, and this number will undoubtedly grow. Recently it was discovered that various molluscs are immune to cancer and may be valuable to research in developing a cure for that disease. While a tangible value cannot be placed on the snail darter or Maryland darter today, perhaps a direct beneficial use of these and other endangered species will be discovered and cherished in the future.

A more vital reason for protecting a vulnerable species is based on its importance in the ecosystem and web of life. Ecologists are only beginning to unravel the complex relationships between living organisms and the environment. Such well-known symbiotic associations as pollination of flowers by bees or the free ride of the tick bird on a rhino's back are only two visible examples of millions of interlocking niches in the biological world. The loss of one species can lead to a chain reaction of impacts upon its predators, its prey, and its associates as well as to the physical environment.

The outcome of man's tampering often unveils the subtle balance of the stable, natural world. For example, the introduction of the Norway rat into the United States has reduced the black rat to rarity. During the nineteenth century, the wholesale extermination of the eastern cougar (*Felis concolor couguar*) and the gray wolf (*Canis lupus lycacon*) contributed to overpopulation of the white-tailed deer in some areas. In a more subtle example, the destruction of Chesapeake marshland by bulldozers eliminates nursery grounds for the very fish consumed by shoreline developers and their families. The diversity of the world's ecosystem is only exceeded by its complexity.

When the Tecopa pupfish was declared extinct in November 1981 because its native stream in Death Valley, California, was altered to provide spring water for bathhouses, the diversity of North American wildlife diminished. When this species vanished, not only did its untapped biological potential escape our grasp forever, but its contribution to the stability of the world's ecosystem was lost as well. Yet because of man, it perished; and this North American native joined the ranks of the Steller's sea cow (1768), the great auk (1844), and the Socorro snail (1971), all lost for all of time.

From this evidence it is clear that the rate of modern day extinctions serves as a barometer for the health of the environment. And the number of endangered species in this country and in this region sets an unfortunate benchmark for the decade. Without exaggeration it may be said that the accelerating rate of man-caused extinctions is threatening the diversity and, hence ultimately, the quality of life on earth.

THE ENDANGERED SPECIES PROGRAM

On December 28, 1973, Congress voted into law the Endangered Species Act of 1973 "to provide a means whereby the ecosystems upon which endangered species and threatened species depend may be conserved" and "to provide a program for the conservation of such endangered species and threatened species." Although the original Act applied only to members of the animal kingdom, subsequent amendments have added endangered and threatened plants to the national program administered by the U. S. Fish and Wildlife Service and the National Marine Fisheries Service. In the case of marine species, the National Marine Fisheries Service has either shared (e.g., for sea turtles) or sole (e.g., for whales) jurisdiction.

In addition to interagency consultation on federal projects that may affect protected species, the program provides a listing process for "endangered" and "threatened" species, designates critical habitat for some of the listed biota, and protects endangered species through prohibitions including a ban on the taking of wildlife (e.g., capture, harassment, killing, or commercial trade of protected species).

In an effort to restore endangered populations to stable status, recovery plans are drafted and implemented. Management techniques include restoration of habitat, land acquisition, translocation of populations, and captive breeding. Recovery plans are being implemented or are under preparation for the gray myotis, Indiana myotis, Virginia big-eared bat, Delmarva fox squirrel, eastern cougar, brown pelican, bald eagle, peregrine falcon, red-cockaded woodpecker, Kirtland's warbler, the sea turtles, shortnose sturgeon, Maryland darter, Virginia fringed mountain snail, the mussels of the Clinch and Powell rivers, and the Virginia round-leaf birch, among others.

On the international level, the federal government is a partner in various migratory bird and marine mammal treaties. In addition, the United States is a member of the Convention on International Trade in Endangered Species of Wild Fauna and Flora (CITES), a treaty signed in 1973, that requires each of nearly 70 member nations to adopt strict controls over the import and export of species that have been endangered, at least in part, by international trade.

Within local political boundaries, the states of Delaware, Maryland, and Virginia have signed cooperative agreements with the federal government, and these states have promulgated laws that protect resident populations of jeopardized wildlife. The responsible state agencies play an essential part in the implementation of recovery efforts for endangered species.

THE CHESAPEAKE BAY WATERSHED AND OHIO RIVER BASIN

As the largest and most productive estuary in the United States, the Chesapeake Bay dominates the middle Atlantic coast. Its watershed (64,000 square miles) encompasses most of Maryland, Virginia, central Pennsylvania, and southwestern Delaware. From the source of the Susquehanna in New York State to the mouth of the Bay between Cape Charles and Cape Henry, the length of the watershed is over 650 miles.

The Bay proper spans 195 miles from Susquehanna Flats to its mouth and is bordered by 8,100 miles of shoreline including its tributaries. The second major freshwater source, the Potomac River, stretches far into western Maryland, Virginia, and West Virginia. Also on the western shore the Rappahannock, York, and James rivers of the Virginia Commonwealth flow eastward into the Chesapeake estuary. Across the Bay on the Delmarva Peninsula, the tributaries of the Nanticoke and Pocomoke rivers originate in Delaware.

West of the Appalachian divide, the waters of Maryland flow directly into tributaries of the Ohio River, while southwestern Virginia is drained by the Cumberland, Tennessee, and Ohio river systems. The Cumberland and Tennessee rivers join the Ohio before its confluence with the Mississippi.

The multitude of habitat types in the states of Delaware, Maryland, and Virginia are discussed appropriately in the introductions to each animal and plant group. Although the variety of habitats is extensive, the total acreages of many types have been declining for centuries. For this reason, habitat loss is the primary threat to endangered terrestrial wildlife in the region. The aquatic biota is also imperiled by the loss of habitat in the Chesapeake Bay, the Ohio River Basin, and their tributaries, *directly* through wetlands destruction and the building of dams and *indirectly* from the effects of waterborne pollution.

Section I

Endangered and Threatened Wildlife in the Tri-State Region

MAMMALS THREATENED WITH EXTINCTION

From the birch and oak-hickory forests of the Blue Ridge Mountains to the cordgrass marshes of the Chesapeake Bay, a diversity of habitats has been colonized by the mammalian fauna of Delaware, Maryland, and Virginia. Today over 75 species of mammals inhabit these states and their coastal waters. Before European settlers first stepped on Virginia soil 350 years ago, many other species, including the bison, elk, gray wolf, manatee, and fisher populated the region. During the eighteenth and nineteenth centuries, hunting, the destruction of habitat, and the encroachment of civilization resulted in the extirpation of these animals from the area.

Of the 32 mammalian species and subspecies in the United States endangered with extinction today, 11 inhabit or migrate through the tri-state region and coastal waters. These federally listed mammals, which include 3 species of bats, the endemic Delmarva Peninsula fox squirrel (*Sciurus niger cinereus*), the eastern cougar (*F. c. couguar*), and 6 species of whales, are discussed individually in this section.

In addition to these protected mammals, 4 shrews and 2 rodents with limited ranges are potentially threatened but are not protected by the federal government at present. Population studies are underway to evaluate the status of these secretive creatures and to determine if protective measures are needed for the remaining populations. Here, the range and habitat as well as the reasons for special concern for these rare animals are briefly discussed.

The Dismal Swamp shrew (*Sorex longirostris fisheri*), the swamp short-tailed shrew (*Blarina brevicauda telmalestes*) and the southern bog lemming (*Synaptomys cooperi helaletes*) are all endemic to the Dismal Swamp in southeastern Virginia and northeastern North Carolina. The preferred habitats of the two shrews are cane brakes and swamp thickets as well as grassy marshes, clearings, and forest. The southern bog lemming is a resident of cane patches and grassy marshes and like the shrews is potentially threatened by habitat destruction.

The northern water shrew (*Sorex palustris punctulatus*), the pygmy shrew (*Microsorex hoyi winnemana*), and the northern flying squirrel (*Glaucomys sabrinus fuscus*) dwell in the hardwood forests of western Virginia and adjacent states. The northern water shrew, which may now be extirpated from Virginia because of the construction of a hydroelectric dam at its one known Virginia site, is also found in Pennsylvania and West Virginia where it inhabits mountain streams and forested stream borders. Of all the mammals living in North America and South America, the pygmy shrew is the smallest, with a total weight of less than 3 grams (about 1/9 of an ounce). This diminutive shrew is found from Maryland and Virginia to northern Georgia in the deep leaf litter of mixed conifer-hardwood forests and in clearings.

A denizen of red spruce and mixed hardwood forests, the West Virginia subspecies of the northern flying squirrel has only been seen in Virginia on the upper slopes of Whitetop Mountain in Smyth County. This glider is on the verge of extirpation from Virginia due to the logging and clearing of the last remnants of spruce-fir-hemlock forests. In addition to these potentially threatened subspecies, a subspecies of the eastern cottontail rabbit (*Silvilagus floridanus hitchensi*), if it still exists, may be in danger of extinction. An insular subspecies found on Smith and Fisherman islands in Northampton County, Virginia, prior to 1910, this rabbit may not have survived a hurricane in 1933. Therefore, its status remains undetermined.

With the exception of the large whales and eastern cougar, the endangered mammals of the region are habitat specialists with small geographic ranges. Some of these mammals such as the Delmarva Peninsula fox squirrel formerly had much larger ranges. Others, for example the Virginia big-eared bat (*Plecotus townsendii virginianus*), occupy small, isolated ranges which probably never were large or continuous.

The tendency of these endangered mammals to depend on isolated niches makes them particularly susceptible to population reductions from the consequences of habitat destruction by man. The 3 endangered bats, the gray myotis (*Myotis grisescens*), the Indiana myotis (*Myotis sodalis*), and the Virginia big-eared bat are cave dwellers and easily disturbed by spelunkers and unfavorable alterations to cave entrances. Among the potentially threatened species, the southern bog lemming and the 2 shrews endemic to Dismal Swamp and isolated habitats therein are threatened by swamp draining and channelization. For forest dwellers the impact of man is easily demonstrated. The Delmarva Peninsula fox squirrel previously occupied the conifer and mixed hardwood forests that spanned the entire Delmarva Peninsula into southern Pennsylvania and New Jersey before most of this timber was cleared to create farmland. Today this protected native is only found in isolated stands of mature conifers and hardwoods on the Eastern Shore of Maryland and has been introduced successfully onto Assateague Island, Virginia, in the Chincoteague National Wildlife Refuge.

While hunting has been of minor consideration in the endangerment of the Delmarva Peninsula fox squirrel population, commercial whaling is the most important reason for the endangerment of the sperm whale (*Physeter catodon*) and the 5 baleen whales of the North Atlantic.

Due to extermination by farmers seeking to protect their livestock, the eastern cougar was probably extirpated from this region in or soon after 1882 (the date of the last reported kill in Virginia). In the late 1960s through the 1970s, however, fairly reliable sightings of "cougars" in Maryland and Virginia have been reported. Whether these sightings are of the eastern cougar (*F. c. couguar*) or a released subspecies of western cougar, is unknown at this time.

Besides the threat of habitat disturbance, the insectivorous bats and shrews may also be threatened by the use of pesticides in agriculture. For example, in research studies completed at Patuxent Wildlife Research Center, Maryland, mortality in the gray myotis was linked to lethal quantities of the insecticide dieldrin.

Ranging from the smallest pygmy shrew to the largest of mammals, the blue whale (*Balaenoptera musculus*), more than 20 percent of the mammalian fauna of this region is endangered, threatened, or potentially threatened. Complete accounts follow for the federally protected species, while little is currently known about the status of the aforementioned shrews, rodents, and the subspecies of cottontail rabbit (see Table I).

Gray myotis
Myotis grisescens

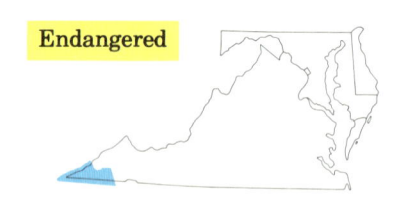

Endangered

Description: This small-eared, medium-sized bat is 2 inches (50 mm) long with a 1-3/5 inch (40 mm) tail, and an 11 to 12 inch (300 mm) wingspread. Dorsal fur is uniformly gray after molting in midsummer and becomes reddish brown by the following May. The only eastern bat with unicolored dorsal hair; underparts are whitish gray and wings are black.

Distribution: Present Range: Summer populations range from eastern Kansas and Oklahoma eastward to southwestern Virginia and North Carolina; from a northern limit of southern Illinois and Indiana, the summer distribution extends to northern Florida. Winter hibernation is restricted primarily to five major caves in Kentucky, Tennessee, and northern Alabama, where more than half of the entire species population (estimated at 1,500,000) hibernate in a single cave. DE-MD-VA: Summer populations that appear to be bachelor colonies are found in Lee and Scott Counties in southwestern Virginia.

Habitat and Behavior: A true cave bat, the gray myotis migrates up to 300 miles between winter cave hibernacula and summer cave maternity colonies and bachelor roosts. At dusk, foraging bats leave their roosts to hunt for mayflies and other aquatic insects over nearby rivers and lakes.

Reproduction: Mating takes place in the fall. Females store sperm in the uterus over the winter, and a single offspring is born to each breeding female in late May or early June.

Remarks: The recent decline of the gray myotis is primarily due to human disturbance of maternity caves and winter hibernacula by spelunkers, vandals, and commercialization. Summer maternity colonies are particularly vulnerable. Shining a light on roosting females or simply entering a cave can cause thousands of young to be dropped to the cave floor. This sensitivity to disturbance coupled with its low reproductive rate and high offspring mortality has substantially depleted most colonies.

Indiana myotis
Myotis sodalis

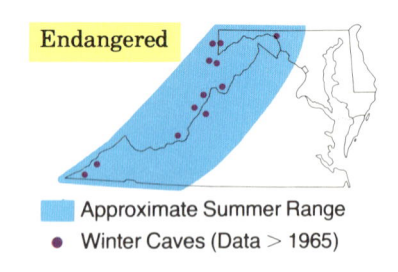

Endangered

Approximate Summer Range

• Winter Caves (Data > 1965)

Description: The Indiana myotis has dark brown hair on its shoulders and dull grayish brown on its back; belly is pinkish white, and wing membrane is blackish brown. Its small, mouselike ears and plain nose are distinctive. Of all the bats that are endangered, this bat is the smallest. The larger females are less than 2 inches (47 mm) long with a 1-2/5 inch (37 mm) tail. Wingspan is typically 10 inches (250 mm) in flight.

Distribution: Present Range: This migratory species is dispersed in summer across the middle section of central and eastern United States from eastern Iowa and Oklahoma to Maryland and Virginia and northward along the Appalachians into Vermont. Approximately 85 percent of the entire species (estimated at 509,000) winters in only 6 caves in Missouri, Indiana, and Kentucky. DE-MD-VA: In western Maryland, the Indiana myotis is found in small numbers in a few cave hibernacula in Garrett and Washington counties. Historically, these bats have wintered in 9 western counties of Virginia, but currently hibernate in only 2 caves in Lee and Wise counties, Virginia. Little information is available about their summer distribution.

Habitat and Behavior: While males usually congregate in caves during summer, breeding females roost under the bark of hardwood trees. The bats emerge at night to forage on flies, moths, mayflies, and other flying insects in treetops and along stream banks. After migration, both sexes "swarm" in and out of the cave entrances from dusk to dawn. As winter begins, the bats hibernate in clusters of 500-5000 individuals.

Reproduction: Breeding occurs in late fall after autumn swarming behavior. Females store sperm over the winter and give birth to one young at the end of June or early in July after nursery roosts are established under tree bark.

Remarks: Apparently the population once numbered over 1 million, but flooding of caves, human disturbance, and possibly insecticide poisoning have caused an overall decline.

Virginia big-eared bat
Plecotus townsendii virginianus

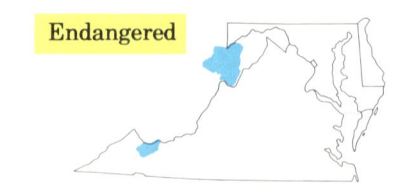

Endangered

Description: With its huge ears and elongated nostril openings, the Virginia big-eared bat is unmistakable. This native bat has brown dorsal fur and pale cinnamon underparts. Similar to the eastern big-eared bat (*Plecotus rafinesquii*), it also has a 12-inch (300 mm) wingspread with black membrane, but its generic relative has blackish pelage and white underparts. A medium-sized bat, this species is over 2 inches (54 mm) long with less than a 2-inch (49 mm) long tail.

Distribution: Present Range: This subspecies is restricted to isolated populations in eastern Kentucky, Virginia, and West Virginia. Perhaps only 11 nursery colony caves are now in existence. DE-MD-VA: Historically, this bat was found in limestone caves in Bath, Highland, and Rockingham counties, Virginia. Today it roosts in only 1 cave in Tazewell County in southwestern Virginia which houses a maternity colony of 200-300 females.

Habitat and Behavior: Although it may move from its main roost to alternate caves, the Virginia big-eared bat is nonmigratory. Summer roosts are usually maternity colonies while males are mostly solitary at this season. These nocturnal bats are agile flyers and dart after flying insects, mainly moths. During winter both sexes coil their ears back against their necks and hibernate in small clusters or in solitary.

Reproduction: After copulation, females store sperm through the winter and bear a single offspring in late spring or early summer. Like other eastern bats, the young are able to fly within about three weeks of birth.

Remarks: The maternity colonies of the Virginia big-eared bat like those of the other endangered bats are extremely sensitive to human disturbance. Females have been known to move offspring after only a single disturbance. Exploration by speleologists and biologists as well as alteration of cave entrances can adversely affect populations. Pesticide contamination may also pose a threat. An estimated 2,500-3,000 individuals are all that is left of this subspecies.

Delmarva Peninsula fox squirrel

Sciurus niger cinereus

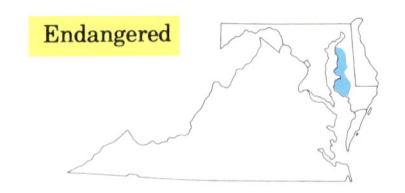

Endangered

Description: The Delmarva fox squirrel is typically whitish gray with a buffy or blue cast dorsally. The underparts and feet are white while its unusually large, fluffy tail has a pronounced black band on the outer edge. The similar but smaller gray squirrel (*Sciurus carolinensis*) has darker fur and a smaller tail.

Distribution: Historic Range: Delmarva Peninsula, southeastern Pennsylvania, and possibly southern New Jersey. Present Range: Restricted to disjunct populations in Dorchester, Kent, Queen Anne's, and Talbot counties, Maryland. A breeding population was reintroduced in Accomack County, Virginia, within Chincoteague National Wildlife Refuge in 1968. Additional reintroductions are currently underway in Cecil and Somerset counties, Maryland. DE-MD-VA: Endemic; same as above.

Habitat and Behavior: Preferring small woodlots with large timber and little undergrowth, the Delmarva fox squirrel is often found in the vicinity of loblolly pines and hardwoods that yield cones, nuts, and acorns for its diet. Less arboreal than the gray squirrel, this Maryland native may venture into agricultural fields where it will feed on corn, soybeans, and other crops. Apparently, these rodents utilize den nests in the winter and leaf nests during the summer.

Reproduction: Fox squirrels have a continuous breeding season with peaks in February-March and July-August. An average litter of 3 young are born and raised solely by the female.

Remarks: Clear-cutting of virgin timber to create farmland and intensive lumbering significantly reduced the range of this squirrel in the 1800s. Afterward, the lumber industry continued to harvest trees at marketable size, and few forests or woodlots returned to the optimum fox squirrel habitat of large, mature trees. Through reintroductions and land acquisition, the Delmarva fox squirrel is now benefiting from recovery efforts.

Top to bottom: Sperm whale, Blue whale, Fin whale, Sei whale, Humpback whale, Black right whale.

INTRODUCTION TO THE WHALES

Although their streamlined bodies and fins give them a fish-like appearance, whales are, in fact, warm-blooded mammals. Whales and other cetaceans (i.e., dolphins and porpoises) must surface periodically to breathe air between dives. Other characteristics distinguishing these more intelligent marine mammals from large fish include their enormous size, longevity (40-95 years), nursing of precocious young, and their horizontal, rather than vertical, tail flukes.

Of the 6 endangered whales migrating in the North Atlantic, 3 (the sperm whale, *Physeter catodon*, fin whale, *Balaenoptera physalus*, and humpback whale, *Megaptera novaeangliae*) become stranded occasionally on the coastal beaches of Delaware, Maryland, and Virginia. The other 3 could potentially be found in state waters if they wandered west of the Gulf Stream during yearly migrations between their polar feeding and subtropical breeding grounds.

The cetaceans are taxonomically divided into 2 suborders. The toothed whales, or *Odontoceti*, include the beaked and sperm whales, dolphins, and porpoises. The baleen whales, or *Mysticeti*, have baleen plates hanging downward from the upper jaw in long strips with feathered fringes that filter plankton, krill, and small fish as water is expelled from the mouth. This group includes the blue, fin, sei, humpback, and black right whales.

The United States no longer permits the hunting of whales or the importation of whale oil or other products. However, at least 13 nations, most notably Japan and the Soviet Union, still permit commercial whaling. Despite the authority of the International Whaling Commission to control the harvest of whales, the killing of endangered species continues. The over-harvesting of the great whales for the products derived from their blubber (oil, lubricants, margarine, shoe polish, cosmetics), baleen (corset stays), and, in the case of sperm whales, spermaceti and ambergris (lubricants, candle wax, perfume, and cosmetics), has reduced many of them to the threshold of extinction.

Sperm whale

Physeter catodon

© W. R. Curtsinger

Description: Among the 6 species listed for this region's coastal waters, the sperm whale is the only toothed cetacean. The sperm whale can reach a maximum length of 69 feet (21.0 m) and weigh up to 61 tons (55,455 kg). The body is bluish gray to black above and paler below. An enormous, flat-topped, squarish head contains 36 to 60 conical teeth in the lower jaw that fit into holes in the toothless upper jaw. The flippers are small, the dorsal fin reduced to a hump, and the large flukes are triangular and notched.

Distribution: Present Range: Found in all oceans of the world and in deep coastal waters. Males venture into polar seas while females and young remain in warmer waters. DE-MD-VA: Sperm whales occasionally visit coastal state waters. Several individuals have been stranded on beaches in Delaware, Maryland, and Virginia.

Habitat and Behavior: This deep-diving whale can remain submerged for 90 minutes and withstand pressures at 3,300 feet (1000 m) and deeper. The sperm whale regularly dives to these depths to feed on squid, octopus, sharks, and fish, which it traps with its teeth and then swallows whole. In this deep darkness, it may echolocate prey with audible "clicks." Sperm whales are gregarious and often swim together in groups, called pods.

Reproduction: In the northern hemisphere males migrate to breed with the females in warmer waters during April and May. A single calf is born after a gestation period of 16 months.

Remarks: An annual toll of over 30,000 sperm whales was harvested during the heyday of the whaling industry. Not only was this species butchered for blubber and meat, but the raw products for candles, oil, cosmetics, and perfume were traditionally taken from spermaceti in the head and ambergris from the gut. Probably only 25 percent of an estimated historic population of 2 million now survives.

Endangered

Blue whale

Balaenoptera musculus

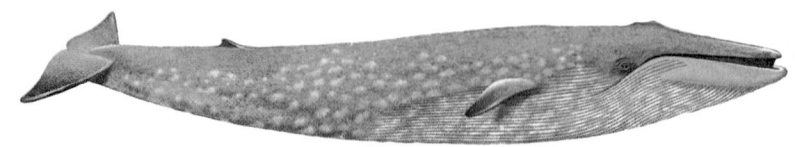

Description: The blue whale is the largest mammal ever to exist on earth. Reaching 110 feet (33 m) in length, it weighs up to 150 tons (136,000 kg). With a slate blue back and white spots on the upper sides and above, it is distinguished from a fin whale in the water by its unusually small, triangular dorsal fin far to the rear. The baleen is black. Underparts are yellowish gray, mottled with white along its numerous ventral grooves.

Distribution: Present Range: The northern blue whale is found in the northern Atlantic and Pacific oceans into the Arctic Ocean, while the southern population frequents the latitudes near pack ice in the Antarctic. The 2 populations rarely, if ever, intermingle because of differences in their seasonal migration times. DE-MD-VA: No stranding records exist for the 3 states, but this species is potentially a visitor in state waters westward of the Gulf Stream.

Habitat and Behavior: While the blue whale is most often found in the deep waters of polar oceans, it migrates to warmer, even tropical, areas to breed. Diving for up to 30 minutes before resurfacing for air, this enormous whale feeds on krill and other plankton by straining sea water through the baleen in its mouth. Usually sighted alone or in pairs, the blue whale may travel in larger groups, which communicate underwater by sound.

Reproduction: Mating occurs during the winter months after migration to warm waters. Females usually give birth to a single calf on alternate years after a gestation of 11 months.

Remarks: The blue whale has declined from a world population totaling over 100,000 to a possibly unviable population numbering between 10,000 and 13,000 today. Unless the current worldwide ban on hunting blue whales is enforced, this rare giant will vanish.

Endangered

Fin whale

Balaenoptera physalus

© W. R. Curtsinger

Description: Although the second longest whale (maximum 82 ft, or 25 m), the fin whale is slender and weighs 70 tons (63,636 kg) at its heaviest while the shorter, 65-foot bowhead whale *(Balaena mysticetus)* may amass 122 tons (110,909 kg). Dark brownish gray dorsally fading to white underneath along ventral grooves, the fin whale can be identified by its tall, curved dorsal fin, small flippers and tail, purple and yellow baleen, and distinctive black lower left jaw and white lower right jaw.

Distribution: Present Range: Similar to that of the blue whale, the migration pattern of the fin whale is seasonal from winter feeding grounds in polar oceans to summer breeding areas in subtropical waters. DE-MD-VA: Of all the great whales, the fin whale is most often stranded on the coastal beaches of Maryland and Virginia. Occasionally visits state coastal waters.

Habitat and Behavior: Traveling in small groups of 3 or more, within loose herds of over 100, the fin whale migrates from polar regions where it feeds on krill, herring, and other small fish to warmer latitudes for breeding. Like other baleen whales, the fin whale only needs to make shallow dives and rarely stays underwater for more than 20 minutes.

Reproduction: A single calf is born to breeding females, which reach sexual maturity at 10 years of age.

Remarks: The fin whale became the prime target of whalers following the decimation of the blue whale population. Even though it is among the fastest baleen whales (averages 14 knots; 20 knots maximum) and rarely swims close to shore, the fin whale still was reduced to 1/5 its former population and now numbers around 100,000 worldwide.

Endangered

Sei whale

Balaenoptera borealis

Description: This moderately large baleen whale varies in color from light to dark gray on the back, is usually spotted on the sides, and is whitish along the throat and the relatively short ventral grooves. Growing to a length of 62 ft (18.9 m), the sei whale can weigh 25 tons (22,680 kg). Flippers and tail are relatively small. Its large dorsal fin does not curve as sharply backwards as does the fin of the larger fin whale. The baleen plates are a distinctive pale gray with white fringes on the fine inner edges.

Distribution: Present Range: This migratory species generally follows the same pattern as the blue and fin whales of visiting cold waters in summer and warmer waters in winter. However, it avoids very high latitudes. Found in all oceans. DE-MD-VA: No stranding records exist for the 3 states, but this whale is a potential visitor in state waters.

Habitat and Behavior: The sei whale is considered the swiftest of the large cetaceans with a maximum speed of 30 knots for short periods. Diving rarely for more than 15 minutes, this whale feeds on small copepods, krill, and fish which it skims with its finely textured baleen and swallows in gulps. The migrating sei whale travels in small groups of 2 to 5 along the coasts or open ocean.

Reproduction: A single calf is born every 2 to 3 years to breeding females in subtropical waters after a gestation lasting 12 months.

Remarks: Since the decimation of blue, fin, humpback, and right whale stocks, the sei whale despite its speed has suffered a recent decline because of its current importance to whalers. More than 20,000 were recently killed in 1 season by Antarctic whaling fleets. Present estimates of the worldwide population range from 31,800 to 75,000.

Endangered

Humpback whale

Megaptera novaeangliae

© W. R. Curtsinger

Description: Like other rorqual whales (e.g., blue, fin, and sei whales), the humpback whale has a torpedo-shaped head, a series of ventral grooves on its throat permitting mouth expansion, a distinct dorsal fin, and numerous short baleen plates. There the similarities end. The humpback whale is stocky or chunky (40 ft in girth) rather than sleek. Only 50 feet (15.3 m) in length, it weighs as much as 45 tons (40,824 kg). Black on top shading to white underneath, the humpback is covered with a variety of knobs and protuberances on its head and extremely long, white-mottled flippers. Baleen is slate gray with white edges. This whale has a humplike dorsal fin and large flukes distinguished by a serrated trailing edge.

Distribution: Present Range: Like the blue and black right whales, 3 distinct populations in the North Atlantic, North Pacific, and southern hemisphere are recognized. DE-MD-VA: The humpback has been stranded on the Virginia coast, but it probably migrates frequently along the coasts of all 3 states.

Habitat and Behavior: Comically acrobatic, the humpback breaches, rolls, and even somersaults with a grand display of waving flippers and flukes. Groups of 3 or 4 probably keep in touch with their dispersed larger herd through sound and "song," during migration to breeding and calving grounds in the Caribbean. Humpbacks are very slow swimmers (3 knots cruising, 6 knots maximum) and rarely dive for more than 20 minutes in their quest for krill, anchovies, sardines, and other schooling fish.

Reproduction: Courtship activities involve leaping, diving, and snuggling prior to copulation. A 1-ton calf is born annually after a gestation of 11 months.

Remarks: Despite international protection since 1966, the humpback has made a slow recovery from its decimation earlier in the century when whalers found this playful swimmer easy prey. Fewer than 7,000 humpbacks survive.

Endangered

Black right whale
Balaena glacialis

Description: Although possessing baleen, the black right whale does not have ventral grooves nor a dorsal fin. This black, heavy-bodied whale reaches more than 53 feet (16.2 m) in length and weighs up to 72 tons (65,319 kg). Underparts are white. It is distinguished by its large black baleen, moderately large flippers, characteristic horny outgrowths, or "bonnets," and the typical V-shaped blow of water and air emerging from its spout during exhalation.

Distribution: Present Range: The North Atlantic subspecies (*E. g. glacialis*) is found from Spitzbergen and Iceland southward through temperate waters. DE-MD-VA: No stranding records exist for this species on mid-Atlantic beaches, but this may be due to its extreme rarity rather than its exclusion from state waters.

Habitat and Behavior: Black right whales are usually found in pairs in temperate waters, often close to island clusters. They swim slowly (3 knots average, 5 knots maximum) and dive for up to 20 minutes, resurfacing to breathe while they lie rather high in the water. These baleen whales feed on plankton, principally copepods, by straining the water. Although seasonal movements take them to warmer regions, right whales avoid tropical waters; and, therefore, the North Atlantic, North Pacific, and southern hemisphere populations do not intermingle.

Reproduction: Little is known about their reproductive behavior, but apparently gestation and suckling each last a year.

Remarks: These mammals formerly traveled in huge herds but now fewer than 4,000 are left. Considered the "right whale" to catch because of its slow speed, enormous quantity of blubber, substantial baleen, and tendency to float when dead, the black right whale has been reduced to dangerously low numbers by man's relentless slaughter.

Endangered

Eastern cougar

Felis concolor couguar

Description: The cougar or mountain lion is a large, tawny-brown cat with a 2- to 3-foot long, dark-tipped tail. Males may reach 9 feet (3 m) in length, including the tail, and weigh 200 pounds (90 kg). Both sexes have whitish underparts. Young up to 6 months old have a spotted coat and light brown fur.

Distribution: Historic Range: Eastern United States and southeastern Canada from Nova Scotia, New Brunswick, southern Ontario, and Maine southward along the Appalachians and coastal plain to Tennessee and the Carolinas. Present Range: Unconfirmed reports and alleged sightings throughout its former U. S. range. DE-MD-VA: Unconfirmed sightings of cougars in western Maryland and Virginia.

Habitat and Behavior: The cougar is not a habitat specialist, but rather requires large, remote areas with abundant prey. Primarily nocturnal, the cougar's former prey in this region was white-tailed deer (*Odocoileus virginianus*) and small rodents, rabbits, and occasionally domestic livestock.

Reproduction: An average of 2 to 3 young are born on alternate years to breeding females.

Remarks: The eastern cougar was probably extirpated from the mid-Atlantic states and possibly the eastern United States by 1899 due to bounty hunting, habitat loss, and the decimation of the deer population at the turn of the century. In Virginia an eastern cougar was last shot in 1882. The persecuted cougar may, however, have survived in the Appalachians and then made a comeback as deer numbers increased. From the number of reported sightings, it appears likely that one or more subspecies of *Felix concolor* have returned to the Appalachians. However, as some experts conjecture, recent sightings may be introduced western cougars; and if that case proves true, the eastern cougar can be considered extinct.

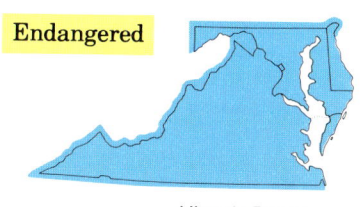

Endangered

Historic Range

BIRDS THREATENED WITH EXTINCTION

The environs of the Chesapeake Bay are famed for prodigious numbers of wintering waterfowl and prolific nesting birds in coastal and upland areas. Since the tri-state area represents the northern and southern limits of many species along the Atlantic flyway, the region has one of the richest bird communities in the country. More than 200 species breed in the mountains and valleys, piedmont, or coastal plain, and approximately 182 species regularly winter in the region.

Among recent North American extinctions, only the passenger pigeon (*Ectopistes migratorius*) has been documented as breeding, albeit rarely, in this region. An enormous colony nested in the Blue Ridge of Nelson County, Virginia, in the spring of 1874. Although this species "darkened the sky" during abundant migrations prior to 1900, it declined to extinction in the wild in 1899. Habitat loss and excessive hunting of the species were responsible. Finally, on September 1, 1914, the last individual, "Martha," died in captivity and on that day this species, which once numbered more than an estimated 1 billion, slipped into extinction.

The heath-hen (*Tympanuchus cupido cupido*), which ranged at least from Massachusetts to the Potomac River, vanished around 1932, and the Carolina parakeet (*Conuropsis carolinensis*), which flew in flocks near Washington, DC, as late as 1865, was declared extinct in the wild after one of the last survivors was shot in Florida during April 1901.

Two northern species, the great auk (*Pinguinus impennis*) and the Labrador duck (*Camptorhynchus labradorius*), the latter of which Audubon claimed to have seen "near the influx of the James River," were last shot and thereby rendered extinct in 1844 and 1875, respectively. Both of these North Atlantic birds may have occasionally visited Chesapeake waters during the fall and winter months.

Currently, there are 68 endangered or threatened birds found in the United States. In Delaware, Maryland, and Virginia, 3 historic breeders, the bald eagle (*Haliaeetus leucocephalus*), the American peregrine falcon (*Falco peregrinus anatum*), and the red-cockaded woodpecker (*Picoides borealis*) are endangered. Bachman's warbler (*Vermivora bachmanii*), which may have formerly bred in Virginia, is also protected as an endangered species in that state, the northern limit of its range. Two other endangered birds, the Arctic peregrine falcon (*Falco peregrinus tundrius*) and Kirtland's warbler (*Dendroica kirtlandii*) migrate through the region, the former regularly, along the Atlantic Coast, and the latter only accidentally. Last, the eastern brown pelican (*Pelecanus occidentalis carolinensis*) is a rare visitor in the coastal waters of Virginia although the nearest breeding colony is located near Ocracoke Island in North Carolina. In all, 7 species and subspecies are considered endangered in the region. The endangered Eskimo curlew (*Numenius borealis*), formerly seen on the Potomac River and along the Atlantic Coast, in autumn, no longer sojourns in the region.

For these endangered species, habitat loss and currently low numbers are the most formidable threats to their survival. The clear-cutting and draining of southern hardwood swamps has nearly wiped out Bachman's warbler. Modern forestry practices that require cutting trees at marketable size have extirpated from many areas the red-cockaded woodpecker, which only nests in pine trees over 60 years old. Invasion of barrier beaches by man has endangered the brown pelican.

The banning of DDT in 1972 and subsequent regulations on the use of other chlorinated pesticides have given many birds of prey a much greater chance for survival. These pesticides can be lethal to eagles, falcons, ospreys, and pelicans, and in the case of DDT, can cause reproductive failure through eggshell thinning. Once again, the bald eagle, symbol of this country, has returned to sustainable numbers on the Chesapeake Bay. Today between 90 and 100 breeding pairs of bald eagles nest in the Chesapeake Bay region, which in itself gives the Bay a special national status.

Eastern brown pelican
Pelecanus occidentalis carolinensis

Description: This huge, dark gray brown water bird has a wingspread over 7 feet (2 m), weighs up to 8 pounds (3.6 kg), and measures 50 inches (125 cm) from the tip of its long, pouched bill to its tail. Adults are white around the head and neck and are unmistakable in flight as they glide close to the water with slow wingbeats and with their long bills resting above their breasts.

Distribution: Present Breeding Range: Atlantic and Gulf coasts from North Carolina to Texas, Mexico, and northwest South America. No nesting records for Alabama or Georgia. DE-MD-VA: Occasional spring, summer, and fall visitor in Virginia, near the Atlantic Coast and the mouth of the Chesapeake Bay.

Habitat and Behavior: Strictly a coastal species, the brown pelican is rarely found inland nor does it venture more than 20 miles (32 km) out to sea. These colonial birds roost on offshore sand bars and barrier islands. Sighting prey while on the wing, the pelican plunges head first into the water to catch menhaden, mullet, sardines, and other fish with its large, pouched beak.

Reproduction: In early spring or summer 2 or 3 white eggs are laid in crude nests, constructed of grass and sticks, on the ground.

Remarks: Although its nesting habitat in Texas and Louisiana was virtually undisturbed in the 1960s, the brown pelican suffered a drastic decline and was extirpated from the latter state during that decade. Like the osprey and eagle, this fish-eating bird is at the mercy of DDT, endrin, and other pesticides. Habitat loss, pollution and oil spills, and entanglements in monofilament fishing line continue to threaten the 20,000 to 30,000 surviving birds.

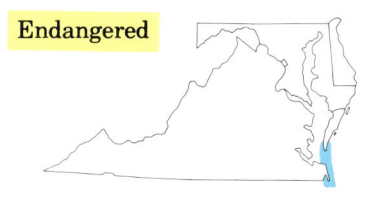

Endangered

Bald eagle
Haliaeetus leucocephalus

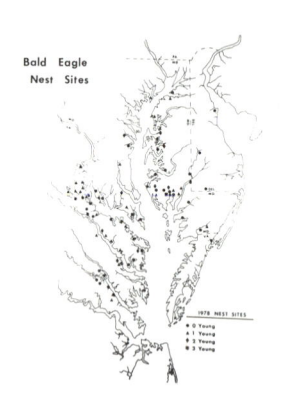

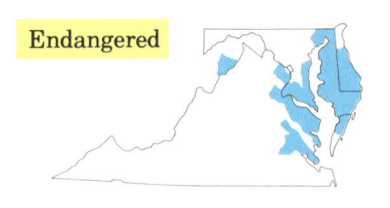

Bald Eagle Nest Sites

Endangered

Description: The bald eagle is a large (30 to 40 in, 75 to 108 cm) bird of prey with a wingspan of over 7 feet (2.2 m). It is distinguished by its pure white head, massive yellow bill, and white tail. Body, wings, and legs are dark brown. Immature birds are brown with white mottling under the wings and tail and on the breast. In flight, wings are flat rather than dihedral.

Distribution: Present Breeding Range: Common in Alaska; range encompasses Canada and continental United States. The species is endangered throughout 48 contiguous states, except in Washington, Oregon, Minnesota, Wisconsin, and Michigan, where it is considered threatened. DE-MD-VA: Found within the Chesapeake Bay watershed and the Atlantic coastal plain. In 1981 a total of 93 active nests were sighted in the Chesapeake Bay region (Delaware: 4; Maryland: 50; and Virginia: 39).

Habitat and Behavior: Preferred nest sites on the Chesapeake Bay are atop loblolly pines within sight of water. The opportunistic bald eagle eats carrion or live prey, including (in approximate order of occurrence) catfish, carp, muskrat, mallard, terrapin, and cottontail rabbit.

Reproduction: Between January and March, 1 to 3 eggs are laid in tree nests an average of 90 feet (27.4 m) above the ground. During normal years, eggs hatch in April and young are fledged by June or July.

Remarks: The Chesapeake Bay region has historically been an important bald eagle nesting area. In 1936, 39 active nests were known to produce a total of 64 fledglings (1.6 young per nest). The use of DDT and dieldrin as pesticides in the 1950s and 1960s caused reproductive failure in bald eagles. As a result, only 7 fledglings were produced in 37 active nests (0.2 young per nest) in 1962. DDT was finally banned in 1972. In 1981, the productivity jumped to 1.02 young per nest; the 1980 index had been 0.85. The Chesapeake bald eagle population is now apparently on the road to recovery.

American peregrine falcon

Falco peregrinus anatum

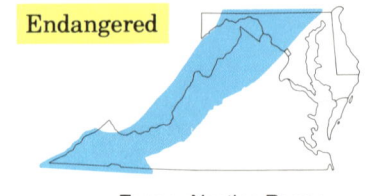

Endangered

Former Nesting Range

Description: The medium-sized American peregrine (15 to 20 in, 38 to 50 cm) has a slate colored back and a reddish white breast and belly, narrowly barred with black. This falcon is distinguished by a thick, black *moustache* on the side of its face. Long, pointed, slate colored wings (3 to 4 ft, 97 to 117 cm span) and a long, dark gray tail marked with black bars further identify this bird of prey. The bill is short and hooked; feet are yellow. Immature falcons are brown above and streaked below.

Distribution: Historic Breeding Range: Southern Canada and the entire eastern United States including the Chesapeake Bay region and Appalachians south to Georgia. Present Breeding Range: Extirpated from eastern United States by pesticide contamination; a few remain in southern Canada and elsewhere. DE-MD-VA: Breeding peregrines formerly nested along the Potomac River and Appalachians. Peregrine fledglings have been recently released, or "hacked," in all three states, principally along the shorelines of the Atlantic Ocean and Chesapeake Bay. Individuals nest on buildings in Baltimore and Norfolk, Virginia.

Habitat and Behavior: Peregrines are primarily found near rocky cliffs, where they prefer to nest. Agile in flight, the skillful peregrine catches prey on the wing. Although falcons fly at speeds of 50 mph (80 kph), they may exceed 200 mph (320 kph) during a long, fast dive (or "stoop") to seize flying pigeons, songbirds, or mallards. Unlike the subspecies *tundrius,* the American peregrine only migrates short distances, if at all.

Reproduction: In shallow scrapes on ledges 2 to 5 (usually 3) eggs are laid. No actual nest is built. Incubation lasts 32 days, and the hatchlings are fledged after 5 or 6 weeks.

Remarks: With the establishment of a captive propagation and release program, young peregrines have been released from various "hacking stations" around the Chesapeake Bay. It is likely that the species will return as a breeding bird in the region.

Arctic peregrine falcon

Falco peregrinus tundrius

Description: The northern subspecies of *Falco peregrinus*, the Arctic peregrine has the same features as the American peregrine except that it is smaller, paler in color and whiter on the breast, and has a narrower moustache on the side of the face.

Distribution: Present Range: Nests during the summer in the treeless tundra of arctic Alaska, northern Canada, and western Greenland and migrates south in autumn, leapfrogging the former range of *F. p. anatum* through the eastern and middle United States, to winter in the Gulf coast and south to Argentina. DE-MD-VA: Migrant on the Atlantic coast of all 3 states; largest concentrations at Assateague Island in Maryland and Virginia.

Habitat and Behavior: In its arctic breeding range, this subspecies is highly territorial, defending its nest site, located on cliffs, river cuts, and slopes, against ravens and eagles, as well as other peregrines. During migrations, the peregrine follows rivers and coasts. With talons ready, this graceful falcon attacks smaller birds while on the wing by striking in a "stoop," or long dive. In addition to songbirds, waterfowl, and pigeons, mammals are occasionally caught on the ground.

Reproduction: In a shallow recess often surrounded by minimal vegetation, 2 to 4 (usually 3) eggs are laid. No actual nest is built. Incubation lasts 32 days, and young remain in the nest for 5 or 6 weeks.

Remarks: Like the American peregrine, this subspecies has become endangered as a result of pesticide contamination. Birds of prey concentrate these toxins in their bodies and brains, leading to death or production of thin-shelled, easily broken eggs. A number of the lethal pesticides, including DDT and dieldrin, are now banned in the United States, but still used in wintering grounds south of the United States.

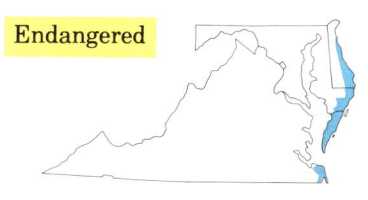

Endangered

Winter & Stopover Areas

Red-cockaded woodpecker
Picoides borealis borealis

Description: A small woodpecker (7-1/4 to 8-1/2 in, 18.3 to 21 cm), this species has numerous white spots in horizontal rows on its black back and wings. The white cheek and black cap are distinctive. Viewed from a distance, the tiny red cockade on top of the male's cheek is rarely apparent. The breast is dull white with black dots on the flanks.

Distribution: Historic Breeding Range: Maryland to Florida and west across southeastern states to southern Missouri and eastern Oklahoma and Texas. Present Breeding Range: Now found from Virginia southward in scattered locations throughout the southeastern United States. DE-MD-VA: Formerly bred in Dorchester (1958) and Worcester (1943) counties, Maryland. Current nesting south of the Chesapeake Bay centers around Sussex County, Virginia.

Habitat and Behavior: The red-cockaded woodpecker nests in cavities drilled in live, mature pines that are at least 60 years old. Only 1 bird roosts in each resin-coated cavity, but a clan of several woodpeckers will colonize a number of cavity trees and defend this territory. Foraging is accomplished by pecking and digging into limbs for ants, centipedes, and insect larvae. Tree and shrub fruits are also eaten.

Reproduction: In Virginia nesting begins in May when the only 1 breeding pair of the clan court and mate. The female lays 2 to 4 eggs in the male's roost cavity. Clan members take turns incubating the eggs.

Remarks: Lumbering and clear-cutting of mature pine forests have endangered this species. Probably less than 50 of the remaining 5,000 to 10,000 individuals are found in tidewater Virginia. The last sighting in Dorchester County, Maryland, was in 1976.

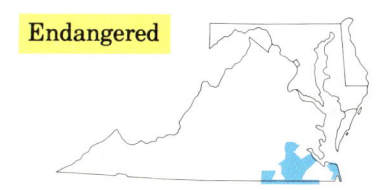

Endangered

Bachman's warbler

Vermivora bachmanii

Description: The Bachman's warbler is not only the rarest, but also one of the smallest wood warblers, averaging 4-1/4 inches (11 cm). Both sexes have thin, needle-pointed bills, olive green backs, and yellow underparts. The male has a yellow face with black patches on the crown and throat. Smaller and plainer, the Bachman's female lacks the black throat and crown. Instead, her forehead and throat are yellow while her crown and cheeks are grayish.

Distribution: Historic Range: The former summer range was the entire southeastern United States. Known to have bred in Missouri, Arkansas, Kentucky, Alabama, South Carolina, and possibly Virginia. Migrated through the Gulf states and Florida. Wintering grounds in Cuba. Present Range: The only confirmed observations since 1950 have been in Alabama, South Carolina, and Virginia. Only individual birds were sighted. It is possible that the Bachman's warbler may now only exist in coastal South Carolina. DE-MD-VA: No recorded nestings in Virginia. A male was sighted at the mouth of Pohick Creek near Ft. Belvoir, Virginia, in May 1954 and again in May 1958.

Habitat and Behavior: The Bachman's warbler, which prefers insects as food, is a rare denizen of southern hardwood swamps and rivers forested with mature hickories, sweet gum, oaks, and black gum. This songbird, which emits a long, flat buzzing trill in one pitch, prefers forest openings with dense ground cover.

Reproduction: About 2 feet above the ground in nests in brush or cane, 4 to 5 eggs are laid.

Remarks: The rarest North American warbler is rapidly declining in numbers. Lumbering, stream channelization, and draining of the hardwood swamps of the southeastern United States are probably the major causes of the songbird's decline. Alteration of wintering habitat in Cuba may also be a problem.

Endangered

Last Recorded Sighting: May, 1958

Kirtland's warbler
Dendroica kirtlandii

Description: The Kirtland's warbler (6 in, 15 cm) is the only gray-backed warbler that persistently wags its long, square tail. The head and back have a bluish gray color, and the back is conspicuously streaked with black. Underparts are yellow with distinct black markings along the sides only. Females are grayer and lack the characteristic black mask of the male. In fall plumage the face, sides, and upper parts are obscured with brown.

Distribution: Present Range: Nests in the north central section of the lower Michigan peninsula; winters in the Bahamas. DE-MD-VA: Occasional transient during fall migrations. Last sightings at Beltsville, Maryland, in September 1976 and at Kerr Reservoir, Virginia, in September 1974. Unconfirmed sighting at Bolling AFB in Washington, DC, during September 1979.

Habitat and Behavior: This warbler nests in loose colonies in stands of young jack pines with dense shrub undergrowth. Tall trees over 18 feet are abandoned for the preferred young pines. Every spring the birds return to this same breeding habitat, which is restricted to an area about 100 miles long and 60 miles wide. A voracious feeder, it catches caterpillars, moths, and other insects with its long, pointed bill.

Reproduction: During June, 4 to 5 eggs are laid in concealed ground nests.

Remarks: The very specific habitat requirements of this species place it in extreme jeopardy. In an effort to preserve the jack pine forest, the U. S. Forest Service regularly burns certain sections since jack pine cones require fire to open. Still, the extent of nesting habitat lessens year by year. Moreover, the habit of cowbirds laying their eggs in warblers' nests has contributed to the further decline of this endangered warbler. Fewer than 500 birds survive.

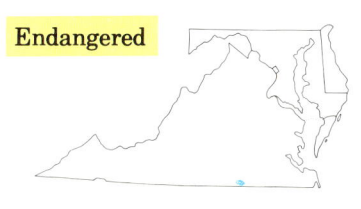

Endangered

Last Recorded Sighting: September, 1976

REPTILES AND AMPHIBIANS THREATENED WITH EXTINCTION

Reptiles (crocodilians, turtles, lizards, and snakes) and amphibians (salamanders, toads, and frogs) are distinct vertebrate classes with very different dependencies on the aquatic environment. Most amphibians spend their egg and larval stages in the water and then metamorphose into lung-bearing adults that can venture onto land. Adult salamanders, toads, and frogs must remain in cool, moist environments, however, to prevent dehydration of their thin, mucus-coated skin. Reptiles, on the other hand, have lungs from birth as well as scales that prevent dehydration. Still, some reptiles, notably crocodilians, freshwater and marine turtles, and water snakes are fully adapted to aquatic habitats.

More than 125 species of reptiles and amphibians have colonized virtually every aquatic and terrestrial habitat in the tri-state region. Since Dismal Swamp and the Potomac River are the northern limit for many of these cold-blooded animals, a greater diversity of reptiles and amphibians, totalling 123 species, inhabit Virginia, while only 89 species reside in Maryland and fewer still in Delaware. Historically, the reptiles and amphibians of the Chesapeake Bay watershed and the Ohio River basin have been widely distributed; and although much of their habitat has been altered, no man-caused extinctions have been recorded to date.

The 5 endangered and threatened sea turtles of the Atlantic coast visit the coastal waters of the region, including Delaware and Chesapeake bays, in summer. The large loggerhead turtle (*Caretta caretta*) is the most common summer resident and the only species known to nest on the Atlantic beaches of Delaware, Maryland, and Virginia. Although this region is a minor component of the species' breeding range, its shallow oceanic waters and the lower Chesapeake Bay provide important feeding habitat for this sea turtle. The less common green turtle (*Chelonia mydas*), Kemp's ridley turtle (*Lepidochelys kempi*), and leatherback turtle (*Dermochelys coriacea*) are occasionally observed in the Chesapeake Bay up to Calvert County, Maryland, immediately north of the mouth of the Patuxent River. The small hawksbill turtle (*Eretmochelys imbricata*) has not been observed in state coastal waters, but probably visits rarely or accidentally.

Out of the 47 species and subspecies of salamanders found in Virginia, 3 are largely restricted to the Blue Ridge highlands and surrounding forest in Shenandoah National Park and the Blue Ridge Parkway. Since they are the only endemic amphibians or reptiles in the tri-state region, these salamanders are the only ones that would decline to extinction if their isolated habitats in Virginia were destroyed. However, all three species live in protected forests, and, therefore, are not threatened. The Peaks of Otter salamander (*Plethodon hubrichti*) is found under logs and wet leaves along Blue Ridge Parkway, and the Shenandoah salamander (*Plethodon shenandoah*) inhabits the rock talus slopes of the three highest peaks in Shenandoah National Park. Their populations are stable and their habitats protected by the National Park Service. The third endemic salamander, the Virginia seal salamander (*Desmognathus moticola jeffersoni*), is actually a subspecies whose population status is undetermined, but which also receives limited protection of its forest habitat for a significant portion of its population in the confines of Shenandoah National Park and the Blue Ridge Parkway.

It is important to note that the only endangered and threatened reptiles in this region are also the largest in size and among the lowest in reproductive capacity. With the exception of the hawksbill turtle (*E. imbricata*), most female sea turtles nest only every 2 or 3 years. Because of this low reproductive rate, the marine turtles, like the large whales and birds of prey, are slow to recover from population declines.

Dermochelys coriacea

Chelonia mydas

Eretmochelys imbricata

Caretta caretta

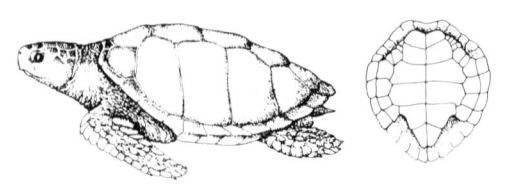

Lepidochelys kempi

INTRODUCTION TO THE SEA TURTLES

Wandering from their tropical breeding grounds, sea turtles migrate northward along the Atlantic coast and into the Chesapeake Bay during the summer months. With the exception of the loggerhead (*Caretta caretta*), the only species known to nest in this region, the sea turtles breed predominantly from Florida southward through the Caribbean and Gulf of Mexico.

Marine or sea turtles, recognized by their large shells and flipperlike limbs, spend their entire lives in the ocean and only emerge onto sandy beaches to lay eggs. The hard-shelled turtles can be distinguished from one another by the number and pattern of enlarged scales on the carapace, or upper shell, and the plastron, or lower shell. Along the median line of the carapace is a row of enlarged scales or shields called the vertebrals. Next to the vertebrals on each side are the costal shields, which are surrounded by the marginals on the outer edge of the carapace. The leatherback turtle, the largest living reptile, does not have scales but is covered with a keeled, leathery skin.

Despite their armored appearance, the 5 Atlantic species are very susceptible to extermination by man. Three of the sea turtles are endangered; the other 2 are threatened in this part of their range. Besides harvesting for human consumption, the major threat to their survival has been residential and commercial development of nesting beaches. Except for the leatherback, the sea turtles are considered edible, if not epicurean, by man. Highly vulnerable upon emergence on sandy beaches, females have been regularly slaughtered by the hundreds for centuries. Even the eggs are eaten in the Caribbean as a delicacy. Defenseless hatchlings and leathery eggs are also preyed upon by many other animals including raccoons, rats, skunks, and crabs. The harvesting of hawksbills for "tortoiseshell" and accidental kills by fishermen and shrimp trawlers have also contributed to the decline of these once-abundant creatures of the sea.

Green turtle
Chelonia mydas

Description: The green turtle is a medium to large sea turtle bearing a brown, heart-shaped carapace mottled with dark brown or olive streaks and spots. The plastron is yellowish white. The green turtle averages 3-1/2 feet (1.1 m) and weighs 300 pounds (136.4 kg). Similar to the hawksbill, it has 4 costal shields on each side of the carapace. However, unlike its smaller relative, the green turtle has smooth, nonoverlapping shields, and has long flippers with 1 claw rather than 2.

Distribution: Present Range: Green turtles are widely distributed between 35° north latitude and 35° south latitude throughout the world. Endangered in Florida and the Pacific coast of Mexico; threatened elsewhere. DE-MD-VA: Immatures weighing 100 pounds (45 kg) or less are uncommon summer visitors in Delaware Bay, lower Chesapeake Bay (north to Calvert County, Maryland), and state coastal waters.

Habitat and Behavior: The green turtle is predominantly a tropical species that migrates across open ocean but prefers shallow coastal areas such as reefs, bays, and inlets to feed. Atlantic immatures wander farther from the Caribbean than do adults. In addition, young green turtles are more omnivorous, feeding on jellyfish, molluscs, fish, and crustaceans in addition to the preferred adult food of sea grasses and algae.

Reproduction: Mating takes place just off tropical ocean beaches from March through September. Every 2 to 3 years a breeding female will mate and lay several clutches of 20 to 200 eggs in nests on sandy beaches. Incubation lasts 45 to 60 days; eggs and hatchlings suffer extremely high mortality.

Remarks: Considered the most valued edible sea turtle, this species has been intensely harvested and depleted throughout its range. Current estimates of the world population of green turtles range between 100,000 and 400,000.

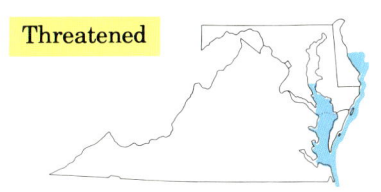

Threatened

Hawksbill turtle
Eretmochelys imbricata

Description: The hawksbill, named for its narrow hooked beak, has characteristic overlapping shields and serrated edges on its oval carapace. Its colorful amber shell is distinctively streaked with reddish brown, yellow, or black. The plastron is white or yellowish, often with black splotches. The hawksbill turtle is small (30 to 35 in, 75 to 88 cm) with an average adult weight of 100 pounds (45 kg). The hawksbill has 4 costal shields and 2 claws on its paddle-shaped limbs.

Distribution: Present Range: Worldwide in tropical waters. Although found in the Atlantic Ocean from Massachusetts through the Gulf of Mexico to southern Brazil, the hawksbill is rarely observed north of Florida. DE-MD-VA: No confirmed sightings although 1 museum specimen is reportedly from the Chesapeake Bay. Perhaps a rare visitor in state coastal waters.

Habitat and Behavior: Predominantly restricted to the tropics, the hawksbill prefers shallow waters within coral reefs, lagoons, bays, and inlets with dense marine vegetation. This turtle is omnivorous. Foods include marine grasses, algae, sponges, sea urchins, jellyfish, molluscs, crustaceans, and fish.

Reproduction: Hawksbill females nest annually between April and November. Several clutches averaging 161 eggs (53 to 206) each are laid on undisturbed tropical beaches during the breeding season. Incubation requires 50 to 70 days.

Remarks: The hawksbill's shell has long been exploited as the source of "tortoise shell" for hair combs and eyeglass frames. Its eggs and flesh are also harvested as food. With reduction of suitable nesting habitat, poachers and other predators, such as raccoons and rats, take a more serious toll. The hawksbill has suffered a drastic decline.

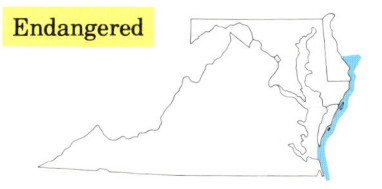

Endangered

Loggerhead turtle
Caretta caretta

Description: Second only to the leatherback in size, the loggerhead has 5 or more pairs of costal shields on its shell. The carapace is reddish brown and the plastron is yellowish. This species attains a maximum weight of 1,000 pounds (450 kg). An average weight of 300 pounds (135 kg) and a carapace length of 30 inches (75 cm) is more usual. Loggerheads have 2 claws on the ends of their paddle-shaped forelimbs.

Distribution: Present Range: Found worldwide in both temperate and subtropical waters. In the Atlantic Ocean major nesting sites occur from North Carolina southward to Florida and the Caribbean. DE-MD-VA: The most common summer resident of the sea turtles visiting state waters. Rarely nests in Worcester County, Maryland, and Accomack and Northampton counties and Virginia Beach, Virginia.

Habitat and Behavior: Crews of oceangoing vessels have observed the loggerhead hundreds of miles at sea, and yet this powerful swimmer migrates far into the brackish water of estuaries to feed. Its diet is also varied and includes marine and estuarine plants, sponges, jellyfish, snails, clams, squid, crabs, shrimp, fish, and other marine animals.

Reproduction: The breeding season lasts from April through September, but mature females mate only every 2 or 3 years. Several clutches averaging 126 eggs (64 to 341) are laid by a female during the summer months. Incubation takes from 55 to 70 days.

Remarks: Although this common visitor in Chesapeake and Atlantic coastal waters has lost much of its former nesting habitat to shoreline development, several of its Atlantic coast nesting sites are now within the national seashore and wildlife refuge systems. Predation by man has also threatened this species' survival.

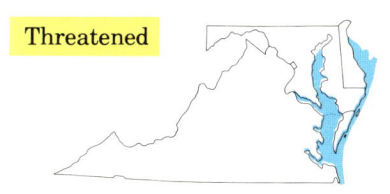

Threatened

Kemp's ridley turtle

Lepidochelys kempii

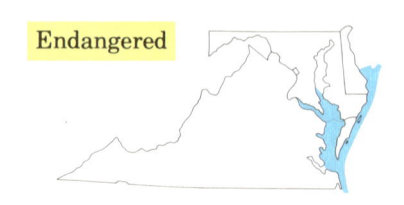

Endangered

Description: The Kemp's ridley turtle is one of the smallest sea turtles, weighing from 77 to 93 pounds (35 to 42 kg) and bearing a carapace of 24 to 30 inches (64 to 77 cm). Its triangular head and hooked beak plus its broad, heart-shaped shell, dark gray (juveniles) to olive green (adults) in color, are distinctive. The plastron is white or yellow. The ridley has 5 or more pairs of costal shields and distinctive pores between its 4 or 5 bridge plates that separate the carapace and plastron. The forearm flippers have 2 claws each.

Distribution: Present Range: Today adults are restricted to the Gulf of Mexico, where they nest, and rarely even enter Caribbean waters. Immature turtles range as far north as Massachusetts in summer. DE-MD-VA: Immatures visit coastal waters, including the Chesapeake Bay (north to Calvert County, Maryland) in summer. A recent specimen found in Baltimore Harbor was probably brought in by boat from the lower Chesapeake.

Habitat and Behavior: The Kemp's ridley prefers shallow coastal waters, especially red mangrove bordered shorelines in the southeastern United States and Mexico. The ridley is carnivorous, preferring jellyfish, sea urchins, molluscs, crustaceans, and fish, and only occasionally feeds on plants.

Reproduction: Nesting takes place on Padre Island, Texas, and on less than 15 miles (25 km) of beach in Tamaulipas, Mexico. Breeding females often nest 3 times annually during the period from April through June. Females come ashore in large groups, or *arribadas,* to lay clutches of an average 110 eggs (54 to 185) per female. Incubation lasts 50 to 70 days.

Remarks: Because of its restricted nesting area and the consequent devastation of these turtles by Mexicans in search of food, the Atlantic ridley is the most endangered sea turtle. Despite the protection of the nesting beach since 1966, the breeding population numbers only between 1,500 and 3,000 adults.

Leatherback turtle

Dermochelys coriacea

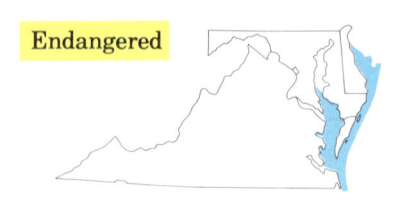

Endangered

Description: The leatherback is the largest of all reptiles and the only black sea turtle. It is easily distinguished from all other marine turtles by the absence of horny plates on its carapace and of scales on its head and limbs. Instead of the usual shelled protection, this turtle is covered by a keeled, leathery skin with 7 longitudinal ridges along the carapace. The large head and back are black or dark brown with white or yellow blotches on the keels and large, clawless flippers. The plastron is whitish and ridged. Total length ranges from 46 to 72 inches (118 to 185 cm), while these enormous creatures weigh from 700 to 1,600 pounds (315 to 720 kg).

Distribution: Present Range: The leatherback's range extends from nesting areas in the tropical Atlantic, Pacific, and Indian oceans to Newfoundland and the British Isles to Argentina and the Cape of Good Hope, and from British Columbia to Australia. Florida is the northern limit of nesting habitat in the western Atlantic. DE-MD-VA: An occasional summer visitor in coastal waters and the Chesapeake Bay north to Calvert County, Maryland. No nesting records.

Habitat and Behavior: This fast swimming species spends most of its time in the open ocean, including cold northern waters, but enters bays and estuaries occasionally to feed on jellyfish, including the Portuguese man-of-war, squid, shrimp, fish, algae, and floating seaweed.

Reproduction: Nesting on sandy, sloped beaches, leatherback females lay clutches of 50 to 170 eggs (85 eggs average) during the breeding season from April through August. Eggs take 53 to 74 days to incubate. Hatchlings and eggs are subject to heavy predation.

Remarks: Due to consumption of eggs by humans and disturbance of open beaches, leatherbacks are now endangered. The current estimate of the world female breeding population is 104,000 individuals.

FISHES THREATENED WITH EXTINCTION

Perhaps this region more than any other in the mid-Atlantic states is known for its abundant fisheries and remarkable aquatic productivity. However, since the arrival of Europeans in the seventeenth century and subsequent deforestation of stream borders, dam construction, and the beginning of commerce on the Chesapeake Bay, many of the more than 400 fish species occurring regularly or occasionally in the region have been depleted.

Because of its size and the habitat diversity within the 5 physiographic provinces of the state, Virginia has the richest ichthyofauna in the region. The 400 species that reside or migrate into Virginia waters include 192 species confined to freshwater, 1 catadromous species, 24 estuarine species, 9 anadromous species, and 174 marine species off the Atlantic coast. Although the estuarine and marine species found in Delaware and Maryland nearly equal those found in Virginia, their freshwater fish fauna (99 species) is not as diverse.

While only 1 fish species (the harelip sucker, *Lagochila lacera*) known to occur in the tri-state region has become extinct since man's arrival, many have declined; and 3 are now threatened in the upper Tennessee River drainage of Virginia. The main factors leading to the extinction of the harelip sucker were siltation, turbidity, and impoundment of free flowing rivers in the Ohio River basin. At present, the slender chub (*Hybopsis cahni*), spotfin chub (*Hybopsis monacha*), and yellowfin madtom (*Noturus flavipinnis*) are considered threatened with extinction for most of the same reasons, although chemical pollution is now added to the list. It is no coincidence that all of these threatened species occur in the Tennessee River drainage. This is a very old and varied river system supporting one of the most unique and diverse freshwater fish and invertebrate assemblages in the world. Unfortunately, it has been greatly modified by man through impoundment, sedimentation, strip mining, and pollution, resulting in an unusually large number of threatened and endangered species throughout the drainage.

In Maryland, the rare and endemic Maryland darter (*Etheostoma sellare*), found only in Deer Creek, Harford County, is endangered. Water pollution and turbidity are probably the major threats to its continued existence. The endangered shortnose sturgeon (*Acipenser brevirostrum*) occurs in very low numbers in the waters of Maryland, Delaware, and perhaps Virginia. Although this anadromous species may once have spawned in the freshwater tributaries of the Chesapeake Bay, the nearest extant spawning site is to the north in the Delaware River. Dam construction on its spawning rivers and pollution are probably the major causes of its decline. At present, these are the only two endangered fish species in the Chesapeake Bay region.

The Roanoke logperch (*Percina rex*), found only in 4 small populations in the Virginia section of the Roanoke River system, the orangefin madtom (*Noturus gilberti*), restricted to Craig Creek in the upper James River drainage in Virginia and the Roanoke River system in North Carolina and Virginia, and the sharphead darter (*Etheostoma acuticeps*), an inhabitant of the upper Tennessee River drainage including the South Fork Holston River in Virginia, are potentially threatened with extinction but are not currently listed by the federal government. These species require clear, free-flowing streams with a minimum of silt and turbidity. The ranges of these fish have been reduced, and their populations continue to be threatened by turbidity, siltation, industrial and urban pollution, and impoundments of formerly inhabited streams. The status of each of these fishes is currently under review by the U. S. Fish and Wildlife Service.

In addition, 2 other species, the roughhead shiner (*Notropis semperasper*) of the upper James River drainage and the rustyside sucker (*Moxostoma hamiltoni*) of the upper Dan River system in Patrick County, are of special concern because they are endemic to Virginia. Although locally common, these inhabitants of unsilted, cool creeks are sensitive to increased turbidity and siltation. For this reason, these species, like the other endemic fish, are vulnerable to a single catastrophic event in their restricted habitats.

Shortnose sturgeon
Acipenser brevirostrum

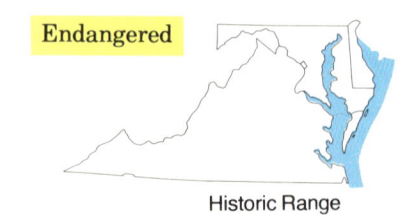

Endangered

Historic Range

Description: The shortnose sturgeon is an elongated, dark colored fish with 4 barbels, or whiskerlike sensory organs, in front of its mouth and 5 rows of protective plates along the length of its body. The blunt triangular head has a very wide mouth located underneath, a typical feature of bottom feeders. Its body is yellowish brown above with a green or purple cast in saltwater. The dorsal and lateral plates are pale and obvious against a dark background. Underparts are yellowish or white. All fins are tipped with white. Individuals are usually under 3-1/4 feet (1 m). At this size males and females weigh about 17-1/2 pounds (8 kg).

Distribution: Present Range: Restricted to the rivers and coastal waters of the east coast of North America from Saint John River, New Brunswick, to Saint Johns River, Florida. Significant populations also spawn in the Kennebeck River in Maine, Connecticut River, Hudson River, Delaware River, and Altamaha River in Georgia, among others. DE-MD-VA: Although a small reproducing population is still present in the Delaware River, the shortnose sturgeon only rarely visits the Chesapeake Bay watershed.

Habitat and Behavior: The shortnose sturgeon is an anadromous fish, and, therefore, migrates from the ocean and coastal estuaries into freshwater rivers to spawn. There the eggs hatch into larvae and remain through the juvenile stage. These fish forage in shallows on benthic, or bottom dwelling, organisms such as molluscs, crustaceans, plants, and insects.

Reproduction: Spawning commences as early as April in the Delaware and Hudson but later farther north. Mature females do not reproduce every year, but, when in season, deposit between 27,000 to 208,000 eggs.

Remarks: The shortnose sturgeon may have once spawned in the Susquehanna and other Chesapeake tributaries, but dams constructed in the late 1800s and early 1900s would have caused its extirpation. Elsewhere in its range, this long-lived fish is endangered by incidental catches by fishermen and deterioration of habitat from pollution, siltation, and dam construction. Overfishing in the past probably contributed to the decline of the species.

Slender chub

Hybopsis cahni

Description: The slender chub is a small, slim minnow, rarely exceeding 3-1/8 inches (8 cm) in length. Compared to other minnows or chubs, it has relatively large eyes. A distinctive black lateral stripe stretches from gill to tail along the numerous scales on both sides of its body. A dark spot also marks the base of the tail, or caudal fin. Adults are olive brown above, silvery on the sides, and white underneath. The slender chub's fins are clear and translucent.

Distribution: Present Range: This small chub is restricted to the upper reaches of the Clinch and Powell rivers in northeastern Tennessee and southwestern Virginia. DE-MD-VA: Found today only in the Powell River in Lee County in southwestern Virginia. The Powell River in Lee County and the Clinch River in Scott County are designated as critical habitat by the U. S. Fish and Wildlife Service. The Virginia section of the Clinch River is protected because changes in water quality in that area could adversely affect the threatened population downstream in Tennessee.

Habitat and Behavior: Inhabiting medium to large, warm water streams, the slender chub prefers stream beds with clean, fine gravel bottoms. This chub feeds on aquatic insects and their larvae in free-flowing stretches of its native rivers.

Reproduction: Its reproductive behavior is unknown; however, spawning probably occurs from May to July, with a peak during the month of June.

Remarks: The slender chub is threatened by an overall reduction in water quality throughout its range. Increased siltation in the Powell and Clinch rivers as well as pollution, predominantly from the coal mining industry, continue to jeopardize the remaining population.

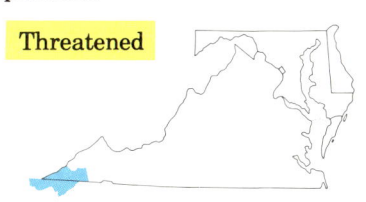

Threatened

Spotfin chub

Hybopsis monacha

Description: A small, narrow-bodied minnow, the spotfin chub is distinguished by its small, laterally situated eyes and a characteristic black spot on the posterior part of its dorsal fin. The body lengths of adults range between 2 and 3 inches (5 and 7.6 cm). Apart from its dorsal and caudal spots, the fins are clear and translucent. Juveniles, adult females, and nonbreeding males are olive colored dorsally with silvery sides and a white belly. The large nuptial males are brilliant turquoise royal blue on upper parts and sides; all fins are tipped with satiny white.

Distribution: Historic Range: Twelve tributary systems of the Tennessee River drainage in Alabama, Georgia, North Carolina, Tennessee, and Virginia. Present Range: Persists in only 4 tributaries of the Tennessee River: the Emory and Buffalo rivers of Tennessee, the Little Tennessee River in North Carolina, and the North Fork Holston River, Tennessee and Virginia. DE-MD-VA: North Fork Holston River (designated critical habitat) in Scott and Washington counties, Virginia.

Habitat and Behavior: Located in clear, warm, free flowing streams, the spotfin chub forages over beds of unsilted small gravel. It feeds on larvae and other immature aquatic insects during the day and perhaps at night.

Reproduction: Its reproductive behavior is unknown; however, spawning probably occurs from May to July, peaking in June.

Remarks: The spotfin chub was extirpated from Alabama and Georgia because of pollution, siltation, and the impoundment of streams. This minnow is threatened in the North Fork Holston River by siltation, chemical pollution, and runoff from coal mining operations.

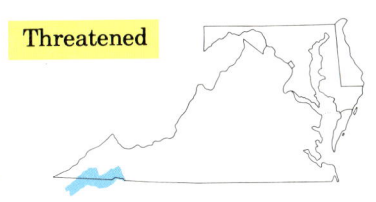

Threatened

Yellowfin madtom

Noturus flavipinnis

Description: This small madtom catfish has large eyes and characteristic "whiskers," or barbels. Rarely exceeding 4 inches (10.2 cm) in length, the yellowfin madtom's body is mottled olive to dark brown with pale areas and fins bearing a yellowish tinge. Four prominent dark saddles mark its upper body, at base of dorsal fin, between dorsal and adipose fins, over adipose fin, and at base of caudal rays. Also, the dorsal and caudal fins are speckled with a pale yellow margin on the outer edge.

Distribution: Historic Range: Collected from 5 tributaries of the Tennessee River: Copper Creek and North Fork Holston River, Virginia; Powell River and Hines Creek, Tennessee; and Chickamauga Creek, Georgia. Present Range: The only surviving populations are in the Powell River, Tennessee, and Copper Creek in Virginia. DE-MD-VA: In southwestern Virginia, this species is still found in Copper Creek in Russell and Scott counties. Critical habitat has been designated in certain sections of these rivers by the U. S. Fish and Wildlife Service.

Habitat and Behavior: This madtom lives in pools and backwaters in small to large warm streams with clear water flowing slowly down a moderate gradient. During the daylight hours individuals remain under banks and other cover along stream margins and deep pools. At night, these fish leave this protective cover to feed on the larvae of aquatic insects.

Reproduction: Spawning takes place in late spring or early summer in native pools or swifter waters. Between 100 and 300 eggs are deposited by gravid females.

Remarks: Considered extinct until its rediscovery in Powell River in 1968 and in Copper Creek in 1969. In Virginia, the survival of this species is threatened by chemical pollution, siltation, and the effects of coal mining operations.

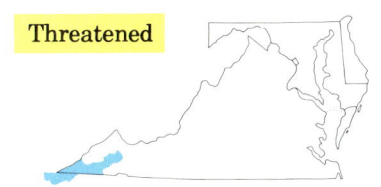

Threatened

Maryland darter
Etheostoma sellare

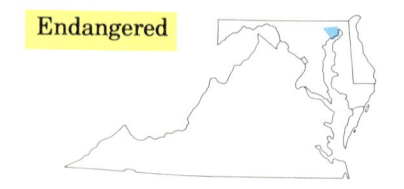

Endangered

Description: A member of the perch family, the Maryland darter is very small, averaging 2-1/2 inches (6.35 cm) in length. The largest known specimen is 2-3/4 inches (7.0 cm) long. This orangish brown fish has dark markings on its head, sides, and pectoral fins and bears 4 distinctive black saddles across its back: anterior to dorsal fin, between the two dorsal fins, at base of second dorsal fin, and between second dorsal and caudal fins. In addition to the 4 saddles, a small dark spot below and behind the eyes distinguishes this species from other local darters.

Distribution: Historic Range: Known only from Swan Creek (1912), Gasheys Run (1962 and 1965), and Deer Creek (1965 to 1981), northwestern tributaries of the Chesapeake Bay in Harford County, Maryland. Present Range: Apparently restricted to a small riffle in Deer Creek, Harford County, Maryland. DE-MD-VA: Endemic; same as above.

Habitat and Behavior; Recently the Maryland darter has only been found in 2 riffles near the mouths of Gasheys Run and Deer Creek. The Deer Creek riffle, which accounts for 100 of the 104 darters collected (80) or observed (24), is 82 feet (25 m) in width and has a substrate composed of rubble, rocks, and gravel. Riverweed (*Podostemum ceratophyllum*) and water moss (*Fontinalis* sp.) are fairly abundant on submerged rocks in the swiftly flowing riffle. Maryland darters feed on snails and larvae of aquatic insects such as caddis flies, stone flies, and mayflies.

Reproduction: The breeding behavior of the Maryland darter is unknown.

Remarks: The extremely restricted range and habitat of this endemic darter make the fish acutely vulnerable to any environmental changes. Water quality in Deer Creek is deteriorating due to high turbidity, nutrients, and siltation from agricultural fields and construction activities. The pumping of water from the creek further complicates the problem of deteriorating water quality.

ARTHROPODS THREATENED WITH EXTINCTION

With over 900,000 identified species, the arthropods represent the largest taxonomic group in the animal kingdom. Over 85 percent of the animals found on earth are spiders, crustaceans, insects, millipedes, centipedes, or their kin, all members of the arthropod phylum. Like the phylum *Mollusca*, the arthropods have adapted to terrestrial, freshwater, and marine environments.

Although there are many other invertebrate phyla, including the sponges, cnidarians (e.g., hydroids, jellyfish, sea anemones), platyhelminthes (e.g., flatworms, flukes, tapeworms), roundworms, annelid worms, bryozoans, and echinoderms (e.g., sea stars, sea urchins, sand dollars), only the freshwater and terrestrial arthropods and molluscs are addressed in this field guide. Nonetheless, it is important to mention that various other invertebrates, for example, the Virginia endemic platyhelminthes, Biggers' groundwater planarian (*Sphalloplana subtilis*), Holsinger's groundwater planarian (*S. holsingeri*), and the Rockbridge County cave planarian (*S. virginiana*), are potentially threatened in this region.

In the continental United States at least 6 butterflies and 2 crustaceans have become extinct in the past 100 years. Currently, among the North American arthropods, 7 insects (all butterflies) and 2 crustaceans (1 isopod and 1 amphipod) are considered endangered, and 6 insects (2 beetles, 3 butterflies, and 1 moth) have a threatened status. Within the tri-state region, only 2 arthropods, Madison Cave isopod (*Antrolana lira*), which is proposed for threatened status, and Hay's spring amphipod (*Stygobromus hayi*), which is endangered, are protected by the federal government at this time.

The Madison Cave isopod, a distant relative of the common pillbug, occurs in only one cave system in Virginia. A shrimp-like creature, Hay's spring amphipod, is a rare inhabitant of a single spring in Washington, DC. These two species as well as the potentially threatened Rye Cove cave isopod (*Lirceus culveri*), and 5 potentially threatened amphipods (Biggers' cave amphipod, *Stygobromus biggersi*; Alleghany County cave amphipod, *S. hoffmani*; James Cave amphipod, *S. abditus*; Luray Caverns amphipod, *S. pseudospinosus*; and Madison Cave amphipod, *S. stegerorum*), are dependent on groundwater for habitat. All of these crustaceans are subterranean species with restricted ranges and small populations, each found in one or two caves in western Virginia. The eyeless, unpigmented cave dwellers are highly sensitive to groundwater pollution and disturbance by man.

Above ground, at least 7 species of insects in the Chesapeake Bay region are potentially threatened although none presently receives federal protection. The regal fritillary (*Speyeria idalia*), a rare and very local butterfly, is potentially threatened throughout its historic range from Maine to North Carolina and westward to Nebraska and South Dakota. Since it inhabits wet meadows and marshy areas, acid rain may be responsible for some reductions. One species of damselfly, *Calopteryx angustipennis*, which is endemic to the Cowpasture River in Alleghany County (Virginia), is potentially threatened due to water quality problems.

Lastly, 4 species of beetles, the sugar maple longhorn beetle (*Dryobius sexnotata*), the ground beetle (*Sphaeroderus schaumi shenandoah*), and the American burying beetle (*Nicrophorus americanus*) and its relative, *N. marginatus*, are potentially threatened in forest habitats in the tri-state region. The tiger beetle, *Cicindela dorsalis dorsalis*, which is found only in New Jersey, Rhode Island, and the Chesapeake shore in Calvert County (Maryland), is also potentially threatened in its restricted beach and dune habitats.

Madison Cave isopod

Antrolana lira

Description: This subterranean isopod lacks pigment and is eyeless. Like other isopods, this species is dorsoventrally flattened and has 7 pairs of leglike pereopods. Its head is rounded in front with 2 pairs of antennae, 1 long and 1 short. Length is 1/2 inch (12 mm), width about 1/6 inch (4 mm).

Distribution: Present Range: Madison Cave, Augusta County, Virginia. DE-MD-VA: Endemic; same as above.

Habitat and Behavior; This species inhabits subterranean freshwater lakes in limestone fissures in the vicinity of Madison Cave. Specimens have been collected that were resting on silt and talus just below the surface of a groundwater lake located several hundred feet inside a cavern. Although little of its feeding behavior is known, this species is undoubtedly an omnivorous scavenger like most other isopods.

Reproduction: Reproductive behavior is unknown. Other isopods have broods of 30 to 50 eggs.

Remarks: The Madison Cave isopod is very rare and is the only freshwater member of its family (*Cirolanidae*) found in North America north of Texas. Like the Madison Cave amphipod (*Stygobromus stegerorum*), this species is only found in a single, restricted groundwater system and is extremely vulnerable to human disturbance and groundwater pollution.

Proposed Threatened

Hay's spring amphipod

Stygobromus hayi

Description: Hay's spring amphipod is an unpigmented and eyeless subterranean species that has been found occasionally in a surface spring. Males are about 1/6 inch (4 mm) long; females are 1/4 inch (6 mm) in length. In contrast to isopods, the amphipod body is flattened laterally, giving the animal a shrimplike appearance. The species has 2 pairs of long antennae and 7 pairs of leglike pereopods, of which the first 2 pair are modified for prehensile movement.

Distribution: Present Range: Restricted to a small spring adjacent to Rock Creek within the National Zoological Park in Washington, DC. DE-MD-VA: Endemic to the District of Columbia; same as above.

Habitat and Behavior: An aquatic crustacean, this amphipod inhabits a portion of a spring that is less than 3 feet (1 m) wide. The spring appears in a rocky wall of the stream valley and flows about 115 feet (35 m) into Rock Creek. Although little is known about its feeding behavior, this species is probably a scavenger and detritus feeder like most other amphipods.

Reproduction: Reproductive behavior is unknown. Other freshwater amphipods average 1 brood of 15 to 50 eggs per year.

Remarks: Construction activities have drastically reduced the number of springs in the District of Columbia. Although a protective fence currently surrounds the spring, construction activities, groundwater contamination, or other disruptions could easily wipe out the remaining population.

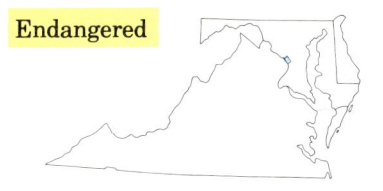

Endangered

MOLLUSCS THREATENED WITH EXTINCTION

In abundance of species, molluscs, which include familiar forms such as snails, mussels, oysters, squids, and octopods, comprise the largest invertebrate phylum aside from the arthropods. Over 80,000 living species have been described. Nearly every environment, including most terrestrial, freshwater, and marine habitats, has been colonized by this ubiquitous group of animals.

Not surprisingly, molluscs have collectively been exploited by man more than any other invertebrate group. In the Chesapeake Bay, the 4 harvestable species, the Virginia oyster (*Crassostrea virginica*), soft-shell clam (*Mya arenaria*), hard clam (*Mercenaria mercenaria*), and Atlantic surf clam (*Spisula solidissima*), have become considerably depleted through overharvesting, although commercial catches remain viable. In freshwater streams, commercial harvesting of mussels for shell has also contributed to the decline of many species.

The phylum is predominantly represented by aquatic species, and, like fish, the freshwater species have suffered population declines to a greater extent than estuarine and marine forms. Freshwater snails and mussels, by definition, are more restricted in range and thus more susceptible to habitat degradation than are marine species. Only 1 percent of the world's surface water is fresh; oceans and coastal bays claim the rest.

Since 1900, at least 9 freshwater mussel species and 21 terrestrial and freshwater snails have become extinct on this continent, predominantly because of man's tampering with delicate riverine ecosystems. Most of these extinctions have occurred in the Tennessee River drainage, which is renowned as the richest center for freshwater mussels in the world. At the expense of these extinct mussels, this river system also supports the largest concentration of dams and strip mines in the country. A somber example of the fate of many mussel populations transpired after the completion of the Wilson Dam on the Tennessee River in northern Alabama in 1924. The flooding of Wilson Reservoir behind the dam extirpated more than 70 species of mussels. Scientists investigated the reservoir in 1970 and discovered the formerly productive mussel bed underneath 19 feet of mud and silt.

Today, 23 species of bivalves (e.g., mussels, clams, oysters) are considered endangered in the United States. All are freshwater mussels in the Mississippi River system and 18 are endemic to the Tennessee River drainage. Tributary rivers in southwestern Virginia contain surviving populations of 8 of these endangered species. The main threats to their existence are siltation from coal mining operations and chemical wastes. The ranges of these species are steadily shrinking year by year.

In addition to the 8 protected mussels in this region, 4 mussels are potentially threatened in the Virginia sections of the Clinch, Powell, and North Fork Holston rivers. These are the acorn pearly mussel (*Epioblasma haysiana*), which is possibly extinct, the little winged pearly mussel (*Pegias fabula*), the fine-rayed purple pearly mussel (*Villosa perpurpurea*), and 2 mussels without common names, *Lastena lata* and *Lasmigona holstonia*. Also, 1 species from the James River, the Virginia spiny mussel (*Canthyria collina*), is potentially threatened as well.

The single-shelled snails include several uncommon and very local species. In the United States, 2 species are now endangered, including the endemic Virginia fringed mountain snail (*Polygyriscus virginianus*), and 5 species are considered threatened. Habitat destruction from lumbering and highway construction has imperiled several of these populations. At least 1 other species, the spiny river snail (*Io fluvialis*), that finds abode in the region is potentially threatened in the upper Tennessee River drainage.

Virginia fringed mountain snail
Polygyriscus virginianus

2 mm

Description: A very small land snail (1/7 in, 3.5 mm across), this species is round in shape and dull white to light brown in color. The spiral shell is compressed flat, and its coiled whorl terminates in an opening that is strongly deflected downwards. Characteristic epidermal fringes protrude from the otherwise smooth shell in a distinctive "comblike" pattern along the whorl. Its tiny eyes are mounted at the top of the largest of 2 pairs of tentacles.

Distribution: Present Range: Known from only 1 locality along the New River in Pulaski County, Virginia. DE-MD-VA: Endemic; same as above.

Habitat and Behavior: The Virginia fringed mountain snail inhabits the rocky bluffs along the New River. It is a burrowing species, and, therefore, little is known about its behavior. This snail probably consumes both plant and animal matter by grasping and cutting with its radular teeth.

Reproduction: The reproductive behavior is unknown. However, from dissections it is apparent that internal fertilization occurs during copulation.

Remarks: One of the rarest and most unusual North American land snails, this species now receives federal protection against both collecting and habitat disturbance.

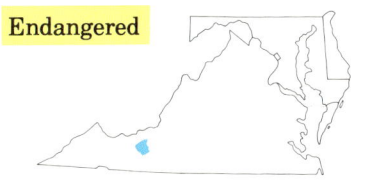

Endangered

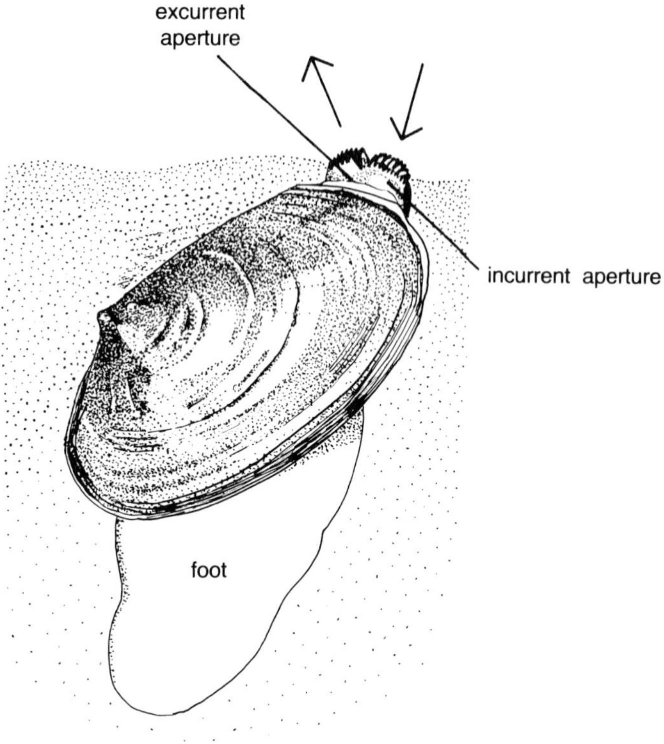
excurrent
aperture
incurrent aperture
foot

INTRODUCTION TO THE MUSSELS

Like other bivalves, the freshwater mussel has a calcareous shell with 2 valves attached by a hinge ligament. The anterior and posterior adductor muscles hold the valves either slightly open or tightly shut. The aquatic mussel is a filter feeder. While the shell is partially open, it draws water through the inhalant siphon and thereby absorbs oxygen and food particles into its highly specialized gills. Filtered water is discharged through the exhalant aperture, which is located next to the inhalant aperture, or siphon, at the posterior end of the shell. The anterior section, including the narrow foot, is often buried in the stream bottom.

Although some mussel species are found in ponds and lakes, the 8 endangered mussels of this region are all found in swiftly flowing streams that provide oxygen-rich water and plentiful food. Moreover, these particular bivalves require a sand or gravel habitat relatively free of silt.

Because of these strict requirements, alteration of native streams has greatly reduced their former widespread range in the Tennessee River drainage. Gravel dredging has directly destroyed bottom habitat in many areas. Chemical pollution, particularly from coal mine spoils and factories, has purged species from certain rivers and stream sections. Excessive nutrients from sewage treatment plants and agriculture fields have often led to eutrophication, and hence oxygen depletion in streams. Finally, the ever-present silt that results from strip mining, coal washing, and improper agricultural practices still flows downstream, settling over mussel beds, clogging gills and causing death.

Hydroelectric dams also disrupt the stream environment in a number of ways. Below the dam, low flows, depleted oxygen levels, and cold water discharges threaten populations. Above the barrier, heavy siltation, resulting from lower stream velocities, quickly chokes any living mussels. In addition, these 8 species cannot survive in reservoirs because of the absence of proper host fish on whose gills and fins mussel larvae, or glochidia, attach for several weeks. Without these host fish, glochidia will not mature into young mussels which fall eventually from the host onto the stream bed. In free flowing rivers, mussels may live from 20 to 50 years or longer.

Appalachian monkey-face pearly mussel *Quadrula sparsa*

Description: This pearly mussel is medium-sized (1-1/2 in, 40 mm across) and has shallow shells, or valves. The brownish yellow outer surface is speckled with triangular green markings and has a pattern of small bumps towards the margin of the shell. The smooth inner surface is salmon to pearly white.

Distribution: Historic Range: Cumberland River, Kentucky; Holston River, Tennessee; and Clinch and Powell rivers, Tennessee and Virginia. Present Range: Surviving populations are only found in the Powell River in Tennessee and Virginia. DE-MD-VA: Restricted to a 15-mile section of the Powell River in Lee County, southwestern Virginia.

Habitat and Behavior: A stream inhabitant, this species requires a sand or gravel bottom and a swift current for survival. The sedentary mussel draws water through its siphon and filters plankton, detritus, and other food particles into its digestive system.

Reproduction: Sperm is released into water by males and drawn into the body of a female through its siphon. Fertilized eggs develop into larval forms, known as glochidia, which, in order to survive, must immediately attach themselves to host fish.

Remarks: The Powell River has been polluted as a result of strip mining and other coal mining operations near the Virginia-Tennessee border. Populations of this mussel were extirpated from other rivers because of gravel dredging, dam construction, pollution, and siltation. Since the Powell River contains the only remaining populations, its continued degradation endangers this rare species.

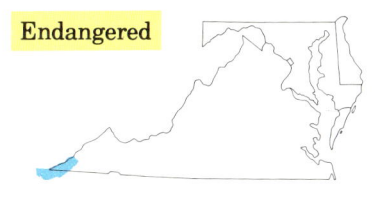

Endangered

Cumberland monkey-face pearly mussel *Quadrula intermedia*

Description: A medium-sized pearly mussel (1-3/4 in, 45 mm across), this species has distinctive bumps covering the surface of its brownish yellow shell. Triangular green markings, resembling chevrons, dot recesses between the bumps. On the posterior ridge of the shell a deep depression forms a small keel. The small interior of the shell is shallow, varying in color from salmon to pearly white.

Distribution: Historic Range: Duck, Elk, Holston, South Fork Holston, and Tennessee rivers in Tennessee and the Powell River in Virginia and Tennessee. Present Range: Still extant in three river systems: Duck and Elk rivers in Tennessee and the Powell River in Tennessee and Virginia. DE-MD-VA: Restricted to a 15-mile section of the Powell River in Lee County, southwestern Virginia.

Habitat and Behavior: This mussel requires fast-flowing water with a gravel and sand bottom. A filter feeder, this animal consumes minute food particles that are siphoned and strained from the water.

Reproduction: Sperm is released into water by males and drawn into the body of a female through its siphon. Fertilized eggs develop into larval forms, known as glochidia, which, in order to survive, must immediately attach themselves to host fish.

Remarks: While the Elk River population in Tennessee has been affected by blockage of river water by Tim's Ford Dam and the Duck River population is threatened by the Columbia Dam project, the Powell River population is primarily threatened by silt and pollution from strip mining and coal washing operations. Like the Appalachian monkey-face and dromedary pearly mussels, this species is very rare in a small section of the Powell River in Virginia.

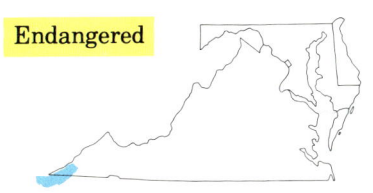

Endangered

Birdwing pearly mussel
Conradilla caelata

Description: The birdwing pearly mussel is a relatively small freshwater mussel. Males average 1-1/2 inches (40 mm) from posterior to anterior edge and have thick, shallow shells; the smaller females (1-1/3 in, 35 mm) have deeper, oval shells. The outer surface of the shell has distinct growth lines, and its variable color ranges from dark green to almost black. The interior of the shell is pearly white.

Distribution: Historic Range: Duck, Elk, and Holston rivers in Tennessee and the Clinch, Powell, and North Fork Holston rivers in Tennessee and Virginia. Present Range: This mussel is now found in the Duck River, Tennessee, and the Clinch and Powell rivers in Tennessee and Virginia. DE-MD-VA: Restricted to the Powell River in Lee County and the Clinch River in Scott, Wise, and Russell counties in southwestern Virginia.

Habitat and Behavior: This mussel is only found in swiftly flowing streams with gravel and sand bottoms. A filter feeder, this animal strains microscopic food particles from the water.

Reproduction: Sperm is released into water by males and drawn into the body of a female through its siphon. Fertilized eggs develop into larval forms, known as glochidia, which, in order to survive, must immediately attach themselves to host fish.

Remarks: The birdwing pearly mussel has always been a rare species. Dam construction, stream channelization, and pollution have all contributed to its decline. The remaining populations in the Powell and Clinch rivers are endangered by the deposition of silt from coal mining operations in the headwaters of these 2 rivers.

Endangered

Dromedary pearly mussel

Dromus dromas

Description: This medium-sized to large mussel is 2-1/3 inches (60 mm) across. The shells, or valves, are solid and typically flattened in small streams (see photo—left specimen) and deep with a more triangular shape in larger rivers (see photo—right specimen). There is a distinctive knob near the hinge. Shell color is yellowish brown with fine green rays. The inner shell varies from white to reddish pink or salmon.

Distribution: Historic Range: Cumberland River in Kentucky and Tennessee; Caney Fork, Elk, Obey, Holston, and Tennessee rivers in Tennessee; and the Clinch and Powell rivers in Tennessee and Virginia. Present Range: Currently found in the Cumberland and Tennessee rivers in Tennessee, the Clinch River in Tennessee, and Powell River in Tennessee and Virginia. DE-MD-VA: Restricted to a 15-mile section of the Powell River in Lee County, southwestern Virginia.

Habitat and Behavior: Like other mussels, this species is sedentary and found in fast flowing rivers and streams with suitable gravel and sand bottom habitats. It siphons water through its digestive system and thereby filters small organisms and detritus for consumption.

Reproduction: Sperm is released into water by males and drawn into the body of a female through its siphon. Fertilized eggs develop into larval forms, known as glochidia, which, in order to survive, must immediately attach themselves to host fish.

Remarks: While the Cumberland and Tennessee River populations are primarily threatened by mainstream dams, the Powell and Clinch rivers populations are endangered by the smothering action of silt from coal mining operations.

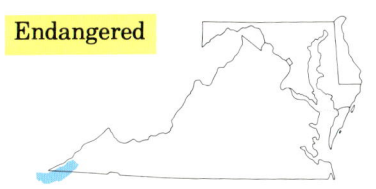

Endangered

Green-blossom pearly mussel
Epioblasma (= Dysnomia) torulosa gubernaculum

Description: This species is a medium-sized mussel (2 in, 50.8 mm across); females are slightly larger than males. The outer surface of the shell has numerous knobs and distinct growth lines. Usually a shiny yellowish green, the shell is patterned with darker green rays. The interior color is white or salmon.

Distribution: Historic Range: Green River, Kentucky; Holston, Tennessee, Nolichucky, and South Fork Holston rivers in Tennessee; and Clinch, Powell, and North Fork Holston rivers in Tennessee and Virginia. Present Range: Today this species is known to occur in the Nolichucky River, Tennessee, and the Clinch River, Tennessee and Virginia. DE-MD-VA: Restricted to the Clinch River in Scott County, Virginia.

Habitat and Behavior: Like other mussels, this species is a filter feeder and a bottom dweller, preferring unsilted, fast flowing waters with sand and gravel substrate.

Reproduction: Sperm is released into water by males and drawn into the body of a female through its siphon. Fertilized eggs develop into larval forms, known as glochidia, which, in order to survive, must immediately attach themselves to host fish.

Remarks: The historic range of this species has been reduced because of dam construction, stream channelization, pollution, gravel dredging, and strip mining. While the Nolichucky population is affected by silt from mica and feldspar mining, the Tennessee and Virginia populations in the Clinch River are primarily threatened by coal strip mining operations.

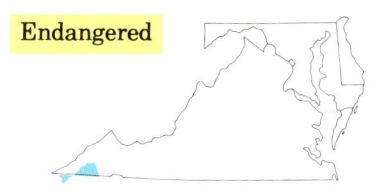

Endangered

Tan riffle shell mussel
Epioblasma (= Dysnomia) walkeri

Description: This species is a medium-sized mussel (1-2/3 in, 42 mm across), which is flattened and rounded in shape. Males are about the same size as females, but the latter develop a prominent expansion on the posterior margin of the shell. The surface of the shell has irregular growth lines with colors ranging from yellow to yellowish brown with fine, light green rays. The interior of the shell is bluish white.

Distribution: Historic Range: Beaver Creek and Red River, Kentucky; Buffalo, Clinch, Cumberland, Duck, Holston, South Fork Holston, Obey, Red, Stones, and East Fork Stones rivers in Tennessee; and the Middle Fork Holston River, Virginia. Present Range: Found only in Middle Fork Holston River in Smyth and Washington counties, Virginia. DE-MD-VA: Endemic; same as above.

Habitat and Behavior: This extremely rare species is found in a relatively silt free, swiftly flowing river with a sand and gravel bottom.

Reproduction: Sperm is released into water by males and drawn into the body of a female through its siphon. Fertilized eggs develop into larval forms, known as glochidia, which, in order to survive, must immediately attach themselves to host fish.

Remarks: This mussel has been extirpated from all states but Virginia, where a small population still survives in the Middle Fork Holston River. Declining towards extinction, this species has been endangered by pollution, siltation, and gravel dredging.

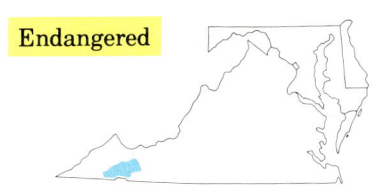

Endangered

Fine-rayed pigtoe mussel

Fusconaia cuneolus

Description: The shell of this mussel is medium-sized (1-1/2 in, 40 mm across) and nearly triangular in shape. With a satinlike appearance, the calcareous shell is yellowish green with broken, dull green rays perpendicular to its distinct growth lines. The valves are deep and solid; the interior color is pearly white.

Distribution: Historic Range: Elk, Emory, Holston, Nolichucky, and Tennessee rivers and Pistol and Poplar creeks in Tennessee; Clinch and Powell rivers in Tennessee and Virginia. Present Range: The species has been extirpated in all river sections except the Powell River in Tennessee and the Clinch River in Tennessee and Virginia. DE-MD-VA: Restricted to the Clinch River in Scott, Wise, Russell, and Tazewell counties in southwestern Virginia.

Habitat and Behavior: Like other mussels, this species is a sessile, filter feeder, preferring unsilted, swiftly flowing streams with sand, gravel, and rocky bottom habitats.

Reproduction: Sperm is released into water by males and drawn into the body of a female through its siphon. Fertilized eggs develop into larval forms, known as glochidia, which, in order to survive, must immediately attach themselves to host fish.

Remarks: The range of this freshwater mussel in the Clinch River is extensive (167 river miles), but the distribution is patchy. Toxic spills in 1967 and 1970 decimated the population for 18 miles downstream of Carbo, Virginia. Siltation from strip mining and other coal operations continue to threaten the population.

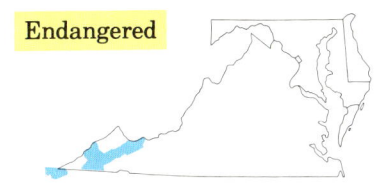

Endangered

Shiny pigtoe mussel
Fusconaia edgariana

Description: The shiny pigtoe mussel is a relatively small freshwater mussel. Its solid, nearly triangular shells, or valves, measure 1-1/3 inches (35 mm) across from posterior to anterior edge. Mussels from the headwaters have shallow valves, while specimens taken downstream have deeper ones. The color of the shell varies from yellowish green to brownish black. Young shells are shiny and are marked with bold, black green rays. The interior is pearly white.

Distribution: Historic Range: Elk and Tennessee rivers in Tennessee; Paint Rock River in Alabama; and Clinch, Powell, and North Fork Holston rivers in Tennessee and Virginia. Present Range: Populations are still extant in the North Fork Holston River, Virginia, the Clinch and Powell rivers in Tennessee and Virginia, and Paint Rock River, Alabama. DE-MD-VA: Restricted to the Powell River in Lee County, the Clinch River in Scott, Wise, Russell, and Tazewell counties; and the North Fork Holston River in Washington and Smyth counties, in southwestern Virginia.

Habitat and Behavior: This mussel is found living in gravel and sand bottom habitats of fast flowing rivers. Like other mussels, it is a filter feeder.

Reproduction: Sperm is released into water by males and drawn into the body of a female through its siphon. Fertilized eggs develop into larval forms, known as glochidia, which, in order to survive, must immediately attach themselves to host fish.

Remarks: Environmental degradation presents a serious threat to this species. The shiny pigtoe mussel was eliminated from part of the North Fork Holston River because of chloride and mercury wastes and from a section of the Clinch River by other toxic spills. The Powell River population is threatened by the smothering action of silt from coal mining operations.

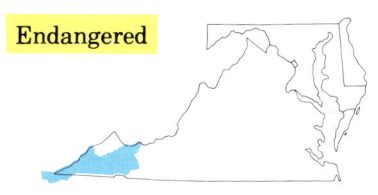

Endangered

PLANTS THREATENED WITH EXTINCTION

While most terrestrial animal species are dispersed according to particular plant communities, the occurrence of plants is more directly influenced by historical distribution, physical geography, and climate. The geographic profile of the tri-state region extends from the Appalachian Mountains in the west, across the Ridge and Valley, Blue Ridge, and Piedmont provinces of Maryland and Virginia, and into the Coastal Plain of all 3 states. Over 2,500 plant species are found in these 5 physiographic provinces, and a number of the endemic, disjunct, peripheral, and scarce plants occurring within them are true botanical rarities.

Habitat alteration and the greed of collectors have placed many taxa in jeopardy. As evidenced by the proposed endangered small whorled pogonia (*Isotria medeoloides*), development, urbanization, and other forms of habitat destruction can quickly reduce rare plants to the edge of extinction. The endangered and endemic Virginia round-leaf birch (*Betula uber*) is threatened by its extremely limited distribution.

Although only 53 plant species are considered endangered and 8 species considered threatened in the United States at this time, hundreds of potentially threatened plant species are currently under review for federal protection. Forty-eight of these potentially threatened plant species occur or have been known to occur in the tri-state area. Because plants are totally dependent on fixed geological and biological factors, habitat destruction usually spells permanent extirpation from a locality or extinction. Recovery is usually slow or nonexistent. The 48 plants listed in Table I are currently under review (as listed in "Review of Plant Taxa for Listing as Endangered or Threatened Species" in *Federal Register* 45(242):82480-82569) to determine their status with regard to their inclusion on the federal list of endangered and threatened species.

Although space in this field guide does not allow lengthy discussion of the hazards threatening the survival of each species listed in Table I, a few examples illustrate their proximity to extinction. The leather flower (*Clematis viticaulis*), mountain pimpernel (*Pseudotaenidia montana*), and pussytoes ragwort (*Senecio antennariifolius*), endemic to the shale barrens of the central Appalachians, are vulnerable to development, logging, and road construction. These and other mountain species, which occur on isolated mountain tops or in forest habitats, have been extirpated from parts of their former ranges.

Although the Piedmont is relatively poor in plant taxa, the mountains and Coastal Plain are richer floristically, and thus the areas where most potentially threatened species reside. In the Coastal Plain most rare and declining species are aquatic inhabitants of bogs, wet meadows, marshes, or tidal shores. These habitats are threatened by commercial and residential development, spoil disposal and filling, stream channelization, and other forms of bog and marsh drainage. Many of these aquatic species occur in disjunct populations since bogs and marshes, themselves, are often isolated and discontinuous. For example, Long's bitter-cress (*Cardamine longii*), a salt marsh species, and swamp pink (*Helonia bullata*), found in bogs and swamps, are now extirpated from their Delaware and Maryland localities and only survive in Virginia. Further evidence of shoreline destruction is the 40-year absence of Long's stargrass (*Hypoxis longii*) and water-hyssop (*Bacopa simulans*) from the Chesapeake Bay environs. These species are now extirpated and possibly extinct.

Small whorled pogonia
Isotria medeoloides

Description: The small whorled pogonia, a member of the orchid family, has a greenish white stem, bearing 2 small alternate leaves at the base. A single whorl of 5 or 6 green leaves surrounds the stem below the flower, which is greenish yellow when in bloom. The sepals are 1 to 1.5 times as long as the petals. The related whorled pogonia (*I. verticillata*) can be distinguished by its absence of leaves near the base, its brown purple sepals, which are 2 to 3 times as long as the petals, and by a peduncle longer instead of shorter than the ovary.

Distribution: Historic Range: 49 counties in 17 eastern states and Canada from Ontario and Maine to South Carolina and westward to Missouri. Present Range: Found only in 1 county in Ontario and 16 counties in 10 different states from Maine south to South Carolina and westward, including Illinois, Michigan, and southeast Missouri. DE-MD-VA: Known historically from 4 localities in Buckingham, Gloucester, James City, and New Kent counties, Virginia. The only living specimen known to occur recently in Virginia was last sighted in James City County in 1980. The species is now believed to be extirpated from the tri-state region. In Maryland, last sighted in Montgomery County in 1930.

Habitat: This rare orchid grows in acid soil in dry, open, deciduous, or mixed pine-deciduous woodlands.

Reproduction: The flowering period begins in mid-May; however, the species does not necessarily bloom annually.

Remarks: The small whorled pogonia is considered the most local and rare native orchid in eastern North America. This species has declined and continues to be threatened by collectors and habitat alteration, such as the clear-cutting for golf courses, roads, and housing complexes. At present only 470 individual plants are known to exist; more than 70 percent of these occur in Maine.

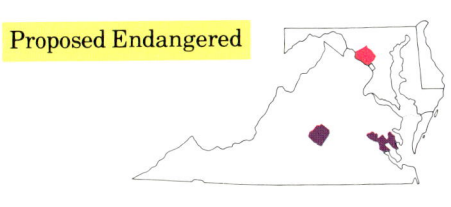

Proposed Endangered

Historic Range

Virginia round-leaf birch
Betula uber

Description: This small deciduous tree, averaging 35 feet (10.5 m) in height, has dark brown, nonpeeling bark which is indistinguishable from that of the sweet birch (*B. lenta*). While large leaves (2 in, 5 cm wide) on mature branches are characteristically round and coarsely toothed, smaller leaves (1 in, 2.54 cm wide) are often elliptical. Like all birches, it bears fruit on a long, narrow cone (see photo at left).

Distribution: Present Range: Restricted to Smyth County, Virginia. DE-MD-VA: Endemic; same as above.

Habitat: The Virginia round-leaf birch is distributed along one-half mile of the bank and flood plain of a small creek.

Reproduction: The reproductive biology is unknown. However, natural reproduction is occurring within the isolated population. Botanists have accomplished successful propagation with root cuttings from the seedling stock.

Remarks: The Virginia round-leaf birch has the most restricted range of any tree in North America. Previously considered extinct, the species was rediscovered in 1975 when 15 trees were found. Now, there are more than 50 cultivated specimens in the U. S. National Arboretum in Washington, DC, but the remaining Smyth County population (approximately 20 trees) continues to be threatened.

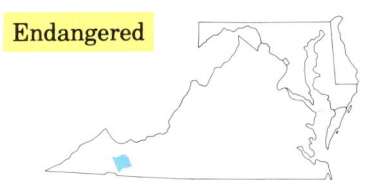

Endangered

Section II

Vertebrates in Danger of Extirpation From the Tri-State Area

INTRODUCTION

The rare and declining wildlife in the Chesapeake Bay region is not limited to nationally endangered and threatened species. Some are in jeopardy only locally. Many animals such as the snowshoe hare (*Lepus americanus virginianus*), sedge wren (*Cistothorus platensis*), and Jefferson salamander (*Ambystoma jeffersonianum*), and plants such as the gray birch (*Betula populifolia*) reach the southern limit of their ranges in the tri-state area. Other species, like the southern bobcat (*Lynx rufus floridanus*), Wilson's plover (*Charadrius wilsonia*), canebrake rattlesnake (*Crotalus horridus* ssp.), and bald cypress (*Taxodium distichum*) approach their northern limit here. These peripheral populations are susceptible to local disturbances of their restricted, and often unusual, habitats. The isolated ranges of many other uncommon species are best characterized as disjunct populations. For example, the bog turtle (*Clemmys muhlenbergi*) has several isolated populations in undisturbed bogs and meadows along its discontinuous, or disjunct, range in the eastern United States. Still other species, such as the grasshopper sparrow (*Ammodramus savannarum*), are widespread in the eastern United States but declining in the tri-state region because of habitat alteration and destruction. Thus, a large number of peripheral, disjunct, and widespread populations are locally rare and declining within the region. These species are said to be *in danger of extirpation* from the region. Yet because these species have stable populations elsewhere, they are not presently *endangered* or *threatened* with extinction.

In contrast to the extinct passenger pigeon (*Ectopistes migratorius*), some former inhabitants of Delaware, Maryland, and Virginia are now merely extirpated and survive in other parts of their historic ranges. In the late 1800s, Bachman's sparrow (*Aimophila aestivalis*) commonly nested in the Piedmont of Maryland and Virginia. This bird and the roseate tern (*Sterna dougallii*), which nested on Assateague Island

and at the mouth of the Chesapeake Bay as late as 1927, no longer breed in the area. The last bison (*Bison bison*) in the region was killed in Virginia on the New River in 1797; the last native elk (*Cervus elephas*) was shot in Clarke County, Virginia, in 1855. Among the native fish, the trout-perch (*Percopsis omiscomaycus*) disappeared from its two regional loca-

Eastern loggerhead shrike (*Lanius ludovicianus ludovicianus*), one of the most critically declining bird species east of the Mississippi.

Bog turtle (*Clemmys muhlenbergi*), one of the rarest and most local reptiles in the eastern United States.

tions, the Susquehanna River and the Potomac River, by 1911. These species were extirpated from the tri-state area because of habitat alteration and over-harvesting, yet stable populations of these species still survive in North America.

In addition to the 41 species and subspecies now receiving federal protection in the region, a large number of native taxa including plants and invertebrates are presently *in danger of extirpation* from the region. The following accounts, however, are restricted to vertebrate animals of local concern (also see Table II).

MAMMALS

Although a number of rare mammals reach the limit of their distributions in the mountains and coastal plain of the region, only 3 are actually in danger of extirpation at the present time. The snowshoe hare (*Lepus americanus virginianus*), porcupine (*Erethizon dorsatum dorsatum*), and fisher (*Martes pennanti pennanti*) all approach their southern limits in the mixed hardwood forests of the Appalachian Mountains in western Maryland and Virginia. These reclusive mountain inhabitants are locally threatened by deforestation, a problem made more serious by the natural paucity of suitable habitat in the southern Appalachians.

Like the potentially threatened northern flying squirrel (*G. s. fuscus*), the snowshoe hare prefers spruce-fir forest, and its original range closely coincided with the distribution of red spruce. During the last century spruce was typically clear-cut; and, after the logs were dragged off, the remaining undergrowth and debris was usually burned. Red spruce has survived in a few damp pockets within birch-maple forests in Virginia and West Virginia where this large hare resides in isolation at the southern limit of its range.

The porcupine has colonized most of forested North America from the edge of the tundra to northern Mexico. However, this quilled rodent is absent from the southeastern United States. The reason for this exclusion is unknown since suitable hardwood forest stretches southward along the Appalachians. The species previously occurred in Virginia and West Virginia. While its southeastern limit is now Pennsylvania, individual porcupines apparently still wander into Maryland. The last documented sighting was in Garrett County in 1967; however, current evidence suggests more recent visitations.

The fur-bearing fisher was extirpated from Maryland and Virginia and the rest of the southern Appalachian states by the turn of the century because of habitat destruction and indiscriminate trapping and hunting. This boreal species ranges southward from Quebec and, like the snowshoe hare, prefers red spruce. The fisher was reintroduced in West Virginia when 23 individuals from the northern stock were released in 1969. The population is slowly increasing and recent sightings are documented for Garrett County, Maryland, and Highland and Augusta counties, Virginia. Similarly, the beaver (*Castor canadensis*), the most important fur-bearing mammal of colonial America, was extirpated from Maryland and Virginia by 1911 but is now re-established in both states.

The Maryland Wildlife Administration has listed 4 rare species in a category labeled "special concern." In addition to the porcupine, the State of Maryland considers the least weasel (*Mustela nivalis allegheniensis*), the bobcat (*Lynx rufus rufus*), and the black bear (*Ursus americanus americanus*) of special concern within state boundaries because of their small numbers and susceptibility to habitat destruction in the western part of the state.

Although no imminent threat places the following species and subspecies in jeopardy, these mammals with peripheral distributions are also considered of special concern because of their rarity throughout the region: the long-tailed shrew (*Sorex dispar dispar*), found in cool, rocky forests in Maryland, Virginia, and other Appalachian states; southern star-nosed mole (*Condylura cristata parva*), restricted to meadows and stream banks in Virginia and other southern states; marsh rabbit (*Sylivilagus palustris palustris*) found in low, wet marshland from Virginia to Alabama; New England cottontail rabbit (*Sylivilagus transitionalis*), an occupant of mixed hardwood forests in the Appalachians including Maryland and Virginia; and the southern subspecies of bobcat (*Lynx rufus floridanus*), a resident of the coastal plain from Dismal Swamp (Virginia) to Louisiana.

BIRDS

In temperate regions such as the Chesapeake Bay, birds are highly mobile, and the local avifauna changes with the seasons. Many northern species, for example, the rare and declining short-eared owl (*Asio flammeus*), winter here, while others, like the endangered Kirtland's warbler (*Dendroica kirtlandii*), merely stop over during migrations further south. As winter approaches, these northern birds, including the Chesapeake's celebrated gathering of waterfowl, arrive at the same time that many regional nesting species depart for the Gulf Coast and South America. This winged mobility allows for fairly widespread distributions; there are no endemic species in the region. Necessarily, the discussion here concerning birds in danger of extirpation is limited to species and subspecies that breed within the confines of the tri-state area.

As previously mentioned, the American peregrine falcon (*F. p. anatum*), roseate tern (*S. dougallii*), and Bachman's sparrow (*A. aestivalis*) are former summer residents that were extirpated as breeding species within the region. The factors causing their extirpation, pesticide contamination, beach and wetlands disturbance, and upland habitat destruction, respectively, are the same three threats that presently jeopardize rare species in the local bird community today.

Real estate development and human recreational activities on the beaches and islands of the Atlantic Coast and Chesapeake Bay have precipitated the decline and near extirpation of several species of colonial nesting water birds and wading birds. The little tern (*Sterna albifrons antillarum*), which nests on the coastal beaches of all 3 states and the Chesapeake Bay (Maryland and Virginia), has declined sharply in recent years. In 1948, 285 pairs bred north of Ocean City (Maryland); none was found in 1977. Only 2 little tern colonies survive in the upper Chesapeake Bay (Maryland) compared to 20 nesting colonies found there in the early 1950s. Little terns were nearly extirpated in the 1800s because of the thousands shot by plumage hunters. Today, only the Virginia colonies (13, Atlantic Coast; 1, Chesapeake Bay (1976)) appear stable for the time being. Similarly the numbers of royal terns (*Sterna maxima*), sandwich terns (*Thalasseus sandivicensis acuflavidus*), and gull-billed terns (*Geochelidon nilotica aranea*) have declined because of modern shoreline development. The piping plover (*Charadrius melodus*) and Wilson's plover (*Charadrius wilsonia*), which were almost annihilated in the region by hunters in the early 1900s, have never fully recovered. Like the terns, the future of these plovers depends on continued protection of their nesting habitat on barrier islands and beaches.

Secondly, 10 species and subspecies of songbirds are locally in trouble. These rare and declining perching birds are threatened by local habitat destruction in marshes, woodlands, or open fields. The jeopardized species (and subspecies) and their nesting habitats follow: Bewick's wren (*Thyromanes bewicki altus*), thickets and fencerows; sedge wren (*Cistothorus platensis stellaris*), *Spartina* marshes and meadows; golden-crowned kinglet (*Regulus satrapa*), coniferous woodlands; eastern loggerhead shrike (*Lanius ludovicianus ludovicianus*) and the migrant subspecies, *L. l. migrans*, hedgerows and edges; Nashville warbler (*Vermivora ruficapilla*), woods and edges; dickcissel (*Spiza americana*), clover and alfalfa fields; grasshopper sparrow (*Ammodramus savannarum pratensis*), hayfields and meadows; Henslow's sparrow (*Ammodramus henslowii susurrans*), broomsedge fields; and swamp sparrow (*Melospiza georgiana nigrescens*), tidal marshes and swamps (see Table II for distributions). In the case of the dickcissel, grasshopper sparrow, Henslow's sparrow, and the upland sandpiper (*Bartramia longicauda*), monoculture agricultural practices, particularly cultivation of corn and soybeans, have reduced nesting habitat and placed the birds in danger of extirpation.

Pesticide contamination, a severe threat to birds such as the gull-billed tern and loggerhead shrike which consume insects, is also extremely hazardous to birds of prey. For this reason, all of the predatory birds, including the goshawk, northern harrier, sharp-shinned hawk, osprey, and the short-eared owl, continue to hold a status of special concern.

REPTILES

While all 5 species of sea turtles occurring in the region are either endangered or threatened, most of the estuarine and coastal reptiles, the northern diamondback terrapin (*Malaclemys terrapin terrapin*), for example, are fairly widespread and stable throughout their ranges. In fact, no endemic reptilian species are found in the tri-state area. However, in upland locations at least 3 species (1 turtle and 2 snakes) out of the region's 63 reptiles are possibly in danger of extirpation as a result of disturbances to very specialized habitats.

The bog turtle (*Clemmys muhlenbergi*) has a discontinuous range from New York to South Carolina. This secretive turtle, which is distinguished by a conspicuous orange blotch on each side of its head behind the eye, is found in disjunct locations in the vicinity of sphagnum bogs or wet sedge meadows in northern Delaware, central Maryland, and southwestern Virginia. Basking in the sun or burrowing beneath the mud surface, these aquatic turtles are rarely seen and only found where clear, slow-moving streams provide a constant supply of cool water. Their unusual native environment has been altered in many localities by ditching and other drainage modifications, pond excavation, filling, and mowing of grasses. Although the turtle is locally common in certain sedge meadows, reclamation of these elevated wetlands has placed the vulnerable bog turtle in some danger of extirpation.

The moutain earth snake (*Virginia valeriae pulchra*), which finds its southern limit in the deciduous forests and fields in the Appalachians of western Maryland and northern West Virginia, and the canebrake rattlesnake (*Crotalus horridus* ssp.), which reaches the northern boundary of its distribution in tidewater Virginia, are also susceptible to extirpation. On the one hand, the mountain earth snake is jeopardized by lumbering operations in western Maryland, and on the other, the canebrake rattlesnake, the southeastern population of the timber rattlesnake (*C. horridus*), is vulnerable to habitat destruction and heavy tolls taken by hunters. The canebrake rattler survives in the Dismal Swamp, its last stronghold in southeastern Virginia.

Besides the bog turtle and the mountain earth snake, the Maryland Wildlife Administration also considers the northern coal skink (*Eumeces anthracinus anthracinus*), a lizard that inhabits rocky bluffs and wooded hillsides in the Appalachian Mountains, and the rainbow snake (*Farancia erytrogramma erytrogramma*), which dwells in the coastal plain from southern Maryland to Louisiana, including the marshes of the Chesapeake Bay, to be "endangered" in the state of Maryland. Although these 2 species are rare and vulnerable in the case of local habitat destruction in Maryland, these reptiles are common in Virginia and thus not in danger of extirpation from the entire region.

Several other reptiles, including the red-bellied watersnake (*Nerodia erythrogaster erythrogaster*), which reaches its northern distributional limit in the Chesapeake Bay (Maryland and Virginia) and coastal plain of Delaware, the northern pine snake (*Pituophis melanoleucus melanoleucus*), which is uncommon in the Appalachians and Blue Ridge of Virginia, the southeastern crown snake (*Tantilla coronata coronata*), restricted to a disjunct population in the Piedmont of central Virginia (north of the main population), and the glossy crayfish snake (*Regina rigida*), found in one disjunct population in Virginia, are of special concern because of their rarity or peripheral occurrence. Information on the status of several peripheral turtle populations in southwestern Virginia is lacking. Only extensive field work can verify the population sizes and stability of the many reclusive reptiles in the region.

AMPHIBIANS

Certainly the most secretive and least documented class of vertebrates in the region is the amphibians. The woodland salamanders (*Plethodon*), which hide under bark, logs, and leaves, the mole salamanders (*Ambystoma*), which burrow into leaf litter and soil, and frogs and toads, which blend into their surroundings, are all difficult to sight and collect. Today, out of 125 documented reptile and amphibian species in the region, a full 62 are amphibians (37 salamanders and 25 frogs and toads). Still, whether some "rare" amphibians are actually scarce or simply hard to collect is often conjecture.

No amphibians are known to have been extirpated from the region because of man's actions. However, 7 salamanders are extremely rare in the region and vulnerable to extirpation as a result of potential threats to their very restricted habitats. The habitats of the previously mentioned Peaks of Otter salamander (*Plethodon hubrichti*) and Shenandoah salamander (*Plethodon shenandoah*) are protected by the National Park Service. Therefore, these 2 endemic species are not in danger of extirpation and simultaneous extinction.

The eastern hellbender (*Cryptobranchus alleganiensis alleganiensis*) is an inhabitant of clear, swift, rocky streams and rivers along the Appalachians from New York to northern Alabama and Georgia, and west to southern Illinois and western Kentucky. In this region the 10- to 30-inch hellbender occupies the lower Casselman River in Garrett County (Maryland) and the Big Sandy, New, and Tennessee river systems in Virginia. Dams, siltation, and pollution (predominantly from acid mine drainage) have apparently extirpated this giant salamander from the Susquehanna and Youghiogheny rivers in Maryland and continue to threaten the remaining populations.

The Maryland Wildlife Administration considers not only the hellbender but also the eastern tiger salamander (*Ambystoma tigrinum tigrinum*), found on the Eastern Shore of the Chesapeake Bay, and the green salamander (*Aneides aeneus*), located in the western part of Maryland and Virginia, "endangered" in Maryland. These salamanders are very restricted in their forest habitats and are in danger of extirpation from the entire region. Two other amphibians, the Jefferson salamander (*Ambystoma jeffersonianum*) and the eastern narrow-mouth toad (*Gastrophryne carolinensis*), are considered "endangered" in Maryland, but are stable in Virginia and thus not of regional concern at this time.

Finally, 4 salamanders which occur peripherally in the mountains of western Virginia are also in danger of extirpation. The pigmy salamander (*Desmognathus wrighti*), the shovelnose salamander (*Leurognathus marmoratus*), and the spotbelly salamander (*Plethodon welleri* ssp.) are all restricted to either Mount Rogers and/or Whitetop Mountain in Grayson County (Virginia). These 3 species as well as the white-spotted salamander (*Plethodon punctatus*), which in western Virginia is confined to North and Shenandoah mountains, are dependent on forest at high elevations which traditionally have been logged extensively.

FISHES

The splendid marshes and submerged beds of aquatic vegetation that have historically lined the Chesapeake Bay are the most important natural resources of the estuary. Without these important spawning, nursery, and feeding grounds, the Chesapeake Bay would not be the country's most valued and productive estuary. More than 208 fish species utilize the Bay during the summer, while nearly 50 species winter there. It has been said that the open ocean is like a desert compared to the Chesapeake Bay, and the diversity of life in the Atlantic Ocean would lessen if the coastal estuaries were to die.

The American shad (*Alosa sapidissima*), historically an important commercial species, serves as a solemn illustration of the recent decline in Chesapeake fisheries. Because of its mobility, it is not in danger of extirpation, but like the hickory shad (*A. mediocris*), it is seriously depleted and, therefore, of special concern. In 1890 more than 7 million pounds of American shad were caught in Maryland. In 1980 the figure was less than 25,000 pounds. This anadromous species, which spawned along the Susquehanna River up to Binghamton, New York, before hydroelectric dams were built in the 1910s and 1920s, is now banned to commercial fishermen in the state of Maryland. The numbers are simply too low to allow a commercial harvest. In addition to dam construction, other possible causes of fishery depletions include siltation, industrial pollution, acid rain, entrainment and impingement through cooling systems, nutrient over-enrichment, loss of submerged aquatic vegetation, overfishing, and the use of chlorine and its toxic compounds for disinfection of sewage wastewater. Unfortunately, the exact reasons for the decline of many fish populations in an estuary are usually difficult, if not impossible, to determine.

At the same time, marine and estuarine fishes are not as susceptible to man-caused extinction or extirpation as are freshwater fishes. Approximately 41 percent of all fish species in the world inhabit freshwater and live in less than 1 percent of the world's aquatic environment. In addition to the greater threat of habitat destruction for freshwater species, many riverine and lake fish can often be more intolerant of chemical pollution and turbidity than are marine species. For these reasons, it is not surprising that only 1 marine inhabitant, the shortnose sturgeon (*Acipenser brevirostrum*) is endangered in the United States compared to 32 endangered freshwater species. Two additional species, the Atlantic sturgeon (*A. oxyrhynchus*), found in the Chesapeake Bay and its tributaries, and the blackbanded sunfish (*Enneacanthus chaetodon*), found on the Atlantic Coastal Plain, are in danger of extirpation from the region. Overfishing, dam construction, and pollution have reduced the Atlantic sturgeon to rarity, while habitat destruction of freshwater vegetated wetlands presents a risk to the Maryland and Virginia populations of the blackbanded sunfish.

In the environmentally stressed habitats within the upper Tennessee River drainage, at least 7 species of darters (Ashy darter, *Etheostoma cinereum*; Tippecanoe darter, *E. tippecanoe*; duskytail darter, *E.* species (undescribed); tangerine darter, *Percina aurantiaca*; blotchside darter, *P. burtoni*; channel darter, *P. copelandi*; and longhead darter, *P. macrocephala*) are in danger of extirpation. Siltation, impoundments, industrial pollution, and chemical spills threaten their continued existence in Virginia. In particular, a 1967 chemical spill in the Clinch River killed off most fish species, including the Tippecanoe darter, in a 60-mile (106 km) section of the river in Virginia.

Three other freshwater species outside the Tennessee River drainage are also in danger of extirpation. The finescale saddled darter (*E. osburni*) is rare in the New River, Virginia and declining. The northern logperch (*Percina caprodes semifasciata*), although extirpated soon after 1938 in the Potomac River, is still extant in the lower Susquehanna River. This small relict population is the last remnant of the northern logperch in the Chesapeake Bay region. Last, the Roanoke bass (*Ambloplites cavifrons*), which is endemic to the Neuse, Tar, and Roanoke drainages in North Carolina and Virginia, has been on the decline since the 1950s. Heavy siltation continues to threaten this rare sport fish.

Like other jeopardized species in the Chesapeake Bay region, depleted and vulnerable fish populations need more than protection to assure their preservation. At this late date, declining species require improvement of the damaged environment to win their survival.

Appendix

KEY TO DISTRIBUTION CODES

(E) = Listed as "Endangered" by the U. S. government
(T) = Listed as "Threatened" by the U. S. government
(PT) = Listed as "Proposed Threatened" by the U. S. government
(PE) = Listed as "Proposed Endangered" by the U. S. government

Geographic Distribution

e = endemic population
e(+ "state abbreviaton") = endemic to area including adjacent state indicated
d = disjunct population
p = peripheral population
r = population within main continuous range of species (or subspecies)
? = occurrence in region suspected but unconfirmed

Temporal Distribution

(for migratory species only; i.e., bats, whales, birds, and sea turtles)
b = breeding population; summer resident
m = migrant; regularly appears in state during migration
w = winter resident
v = visitor; casual or unusual trarsient
(h."date") = historical record and year (e.g., h.1962)
s = non-breeding summer resident

Table I:
Endangered and Threatened Species in Delaware, Maryland, and Virginia

Mammals

Common Name	Scientific Name	DE	MD	VA	Habitat
Dismal Swamp shrew	*Sorex longirostris fisheri*			e(+NC)	swamp thickets
Northern water shrew	*Sorex palustris punctulatus*			e(+PA,WV)	mountain stream borders
Swamp short-tailed shrew	*Blarina brevicauda telmalestes*			e(+NC)	swamp thickets
Pygmy shrew	*Microsorex hoyi winnemana*		r	r	dry, hardwood forests
Gray myotis (E)	*Myotis grisescens*			p,s	caves only
Indiana myotis (E)	*Myotis sodalis*		p,w	p,w	caves, hollow trees
Virginia big-eared bat (E)	*Plecotus townsendii virginianus*			e(+KY,WV)	caves only
Delmarva Peninsula fox squirrel (E)	*Sciurus niger cinereus*		e	e	mixed hardwood forests
Northern flying squirrel	*Glaucomys sabrinus fuscus*			e(+WV)	mixed hardwood forests
Southern bog lemming	*Synaptomys cooperi helaletes*			e(+NC)	swamp thickets
Sperm whale (E)	*Physeter catodon*	p,m	p,m	p,m	oceanic, state waters
Blue whale (E)	*Balaenoptera musculus*	?	?	?	oceanic
Fin whale (E)	*Balaenoptera physalus*	?	p,m	p,m	oceanic, state waters
Sei whale (E)	*Balaenoptera borealis*	?	?	?	oceanic
Humpback whale (E)	*Megaptera novaeangliae*	?	?	p,m	oceanic, state waters
Black right whale (E)	*Balaena glacialis*	?	?	?	oceanic
Eastern cougar (E)	*Felis concolor couguar*		?	?	mountain hardwood forest

Birds

Common Name	Scientific Name	Distribution DE	Distribution MD	Distribution VA	Habitat
Eastern brown pelican (E)	*Pelecanus occidentalis*			p,v	coastal bays and islands
Bald eagle (E)	*Haliaeetus leucocephalus*	r,b	r,b	r,b	coasts, bays, and rivers
American peregrine falcon (E)	*Falco peregrinus anatum*	r,b(h.1940s)	r,b(h.1940s)	r,b(h.1946)	cliffs, open country
Arctic peregrine falcon (E)	*Falco peregrinus tundrius*	r,m	r,m	r,m,w	open areas (mts. to coast)
Red-cockaded woodpecker (E)	*Picoides borealis borealis*		p,v,b(h.1958)	p,b	longleaf pine woods
Bachman's warbler (E)	*Vermivora bachmanii*			p,v(h.1958)	hardwood swamps
Kirtland's warbler (E)	*Dendroica kirtlandii*		p,v(h.1976)	p,v(h.1974)	nesting: jack pines in MI

Reptiles

Common Name	Scientific Name	Distribution DE	Distribution MD	Distribution VA	Habitat
Green turtle (T)	*Chelonia mydas*	r,v	r,v	r,v	oceanic; coastal and Chesapeake Bay
Hawksbill turtle (E)	*Eretmochelys imbricata*	r,v	r,v	r,v	oceanic; coastal and Chesapeake Bay
Loggerhead turtle (T)	*Caretta caretta*	r,m,b	r,m,b	r,m,b	oceanic; coastal and Chesapeake Bay
Kemp's ridley turtle (E)	*Lepidochelys kempi*	r,v	r,v	r,v	oceanic; coastal and Chesapeake Bay
Leatherback turtle (E)	*Dermochelys coriacea*	r,v	r,v	r,v	oceanic; coastal and Chesapeake Bay

Fishes

Common Name	Scientific Name	Distribution DE	Distribution MD	Distribution VA	Habitat
Shortnose sturgeon (E)	*Acipenser brevirostrum*	r	r	r	rivers, bay, and ocean
Slender chub (T)	*Hybopsis cahni*			e(+TN)	clear, warm streams
Spotfin chub (T)	*Hybopsis monacha*			e(+TN,NC)	clear, warm streams
Yellowfin madtom (T)	*Noturus flavipinnis*			e(+TN)	clear, warm streams
Orangefin madtom	*Noturus gilberti*			e(+NC)	clear, warm streams
Sharphead darter	*Etheostoma acuticeps*			e(+TN,NC)	clear, warm streams
Maryland darter (E)	*Etheostoma sellare*		e		clear, warm streams
Roanoke logperch	*Percina rex*			e	clear, warm streams

Arthropods: Crustaceans

Common Name	Scientific Name	Distribution DE	Distribution MD	Distribution VA	Habitat
Madison Cave isopod (PT)	*Antrolana lira*			e	underground cave lakes
Rye Cove cave isopod	*Lirceus culveri*			e	underground cave streams
Biggers' cave amphipod	*Stygobromus biggersi*		r	r	underground cave pools
Hay's spring amphipod (E)	*Stygobromus hayi*		e(Wash.,DC)		surface spring pool
Alleghany County cave amphipod	*Stygobromus hoffmani*			e	underground cave pools
James Cave amphipod	*Stygobromus abditus*			e	underground cave streams
Luray Caverns amphipod	*Stygobromus pseudospinosus*			e	underground cave pools
Madison Cave amphipod	*Stygobromus stegerorum*			e	underground cave lakes

Arthropods: Insects

Common Name	Scientific Name	Distribution DE	Distribution MD	Distribution VA	Habitat
Damselfly	*Calopteryx angustipennis*			e	river banks
Tiger beetle	*Cicindela dorsalis dorsalis*		d		beach and dunes
Sugar maple longhorn beetle	*Dryobius sexnotata*		p	p	mature, deciduous forest
American burying beetle	*Nicrophorus americanus*	p(h.1950)	r(h.1947)	r(h.1896)	mature, deciduous forest
Burying beetle	*Nicrophorus marginatus*		?	p(h.1927)	mature, deciduous forest
Ground beetle	*Sphaeroderus schaumi shenandoah*			e	mountain forest
Regal fritillary	*Speyeria idalia*	r	r	r	wet meadows

Molluscs

Common Name	Scientific Name	Distribution DE	Distribution MD	Distribution VA	Habitat
Virginia fringed mountain snail (E)	*Polygyriscus virginianus*			e	subterranean, forest floor
Spiny river snail	*Io fluvialis*			e(+KY,TN)	swift, clear streams
Appalachian monkey-face pearly mussel (E)	*Quadrula sparsa*			e(+TN)	swift, clear streams
Cumberland monkey-face pearly mussel (E)	*Quadrula intermedia*			e(+TN)	swift, clear streams
Birdwing pearly mussel (E)	*Conradilla caelata*			e(+TN)	swift, clear streams

Common Name	Scientific Name				Habitat
Dromedary pearly mussel (E)	*Dromus dromas*			e(+TN)	swift, clear streams
Green-blossom pearly mussel (E)	*Epioblasma torulosa gubernaculum*			e(+TN)	swift, clear streams
Tan riffle shell mussel (E)	*Epioblasma walkeri*			e	swift, clear streams
Acorn pearly mussel	*Epioblasma haysiana*			e	swift, clear streams
Fine-rayed purple pearly mussel	*Villosa perpurpurea*			e	swift, clear streams
Little winged pearly mussel	*Pegias fabula*			e(+KY)	swift, clear streams
Fine-rayed pigtoe pearly mussel (E)	*Fusconaia cuneolus*			e(+TN)	swift, clear streams
Shiny pigtoe mussel (E)	*Fusconaia edgariana*			e(+AL,TN)	swift, clear streams
Virginia spiny mussel	*Canthyria collina*			e	swift, clear streams
Freshwater mussel (unnamed)	*Lastena lata*			e(+KY,TN)	swift, clear streams
Freshwater mussel (unnamed)	*Lasmigona holstonia*			e(+AL)	slow, clear streams

Plants

Common Name	Scientific Name	Distribution			Habitat
		DE	MD	VA	
Sensitive joint-vetch	*Aeschynomene virginica*	r(h.1899)	r	r	fresh-brackish tidal shores
Aster	*Aster depauperatus*		e(+PA)		serpentine barrens
Water-hyssop	*Bacopa simulans*			e(h.1941)	sandy tidal shores
Virginia round-leaf birch (E)	*Betula uber*			e	stream banks, floodplain
Maryland bur-marigold	*Bidens bidentoides* var. *mariana*		e		sandy flats and shores

Common Name	Scientific Name	DE	Distribution MD	VA	Habitat
Piratebush	*Buckleya distichophylla*			d	streambanks and slopes
Sand reed	*Calamovilfa brevipilis*			r(h.1938)	sandy bogs
Long's bitter-cress	*Cardamine longii*		d(h.1941)	d	salt marsh borders
Sedge	*Carex chapmanii*			d	dry sandy forest
Kearney's bugbane	*Cimicifuga rubifolia*			p	limestone talus slopes
White-haired leather flower	*Clematis albicoma*			e(+WV)	shale barrens
Leather flower	*Clematis viticaulis*			e	shale barrens
Purple coneflower	*Echinacea laevigata*			r	fields and shale barrens
Yellow buckwheat	*Eriogonum alleni*			e(+WV)	fields and meadows
Boneset	*Eupatorium resinosum*				bogs in pine barrens
Wolf's milk spurge	*Euphorbia purpurea*	r(h.1881)	r	r	woods and swamp thickets
Gentian	*Gentiana austromontana*			p	moist, open woods
Pine barren gentian	*Gentiana autumnalis*			r(h.1938)	moist, open woods
Swamp pink	*Helonias bullata*		r(h.1952)	r	bogs and swamps
Lewis' heart-leaf	*Hexastylis lewisii*			p	stream banks and hillsides
Gallberry	*Ilex amelanchier*			?	bogs and swamps
Peters Mountain mallow	*Iliamna corei*			e	open forest
Quillwort	*Isoetes virginica*			e(+GA)	ponds and ditches
Small whorled pogonia (PE)	*Isotria medeloides*	r(h.1944)	r(h.1930)	r	dry, open woodlands
New Jersey rush	*Juncus caesariensis*		d	d	sphagnum bogs
Parsley	*Lilaeopsis carolinensis*			p	shallow marsh pool
Gray's lily	*Lilium grayi*			p	forest openings and meadows

Micranthemum	*Micranthemum micranthemoides*	r(h.1866)	r(h.1938)	r	tidal shores
Bog asphodel	*Narthecium americanum*	r(h.1895)			pine barren bogs
Long-stalked holly	*Nemopanthus collinus*			d	bogs and stream banks
Nestronia	*Nestronia umbellula*			p	sandy river banks
Dropwort	*Oxypolis canbyi*	d(h.1894)			sphagnum bogs
Cliff-green	*Paxistima canbyi*			r	limestone and shale cliffs
Swordleaf phlox	*Phlox buckleyi*		r	r	shale barrens, forest slopes
Orchid	*Platanthera integra*	?			wet meadows
White-fringed prairie orchid	*Platanthera leucophaea*			p	bogs, wet meadows
Rattlesnake root	*Prenanthes roanensis*			p	mixed deciduous forest
Mountain pimpernel	*Pseudotaenidia montana*		e(+PA,WV)	e(+PA,WV)	shale barrens
Mock bishop's weed	*Ptilimnium fluviatile*		p		wet river banks
Knieskern's beaked rush	*Rynchospora knieskernii*	e(+NJ)			pine barren bogs
Sun-facing coneflower	*Rudbeckia heliopsidis*			d	forest borders
Carey saxifrage	*Saxifraga careyana*			p	rocks and stream banks
Carolina saxifrage	*Saxifraga caroliniana*			p	rocks and stream banks
Chaffseed	*Schwalbea americana*	r(h.1875)	r(h.1893)	r(h.1938)	sandy soil, open forest
Bulrush	*Scirpus ancistrochaetus*			p	shallow acidic ponds
Stonecrop	*Sedum nevii*			?	rock outcrops
Pussytoes ragwort	*Senecio antennariifolius*		r(h.1970)	r	shale barrens
Shale barren goldenrod	*Solidago arguta* var. *harrisii*		r	r	shale barrens
Guyandotte beauty	*Synandra hispidula*			r	wet forests, stream banks
Virginia clover	*Trifolium virginicum*	r	r	r	shale barrens

Table II:
Rare or Declining Vertebrate Species in Danger of Extirpation in Delaware, Maryland, and Virginia

Mammals

Common Name	Scientific Name	Distribution DE	Distribution MD	Distribution VA	Habitat
Snowshoe hare	*Lepus americanus virginianus*			p	mixed hardwood forests
Porcupine	*Erethizon dorsatum dorsatum*		p (h.1967)		mixed hardwood forests
Fisher	*Martes pennanti pennanti*		p	p	mixed hardwood forests

Birds

Common Name	Scientific Name	Distribution DE	Distribution MD	Distribution VA	Habitat
Piping plover	*Charadrius melodus*	p,b	p,b,w	p,b,w	beaches and mudflats
Wilson's plover	*Charadrius wilsonia*	p,b	p,b	p,b	beaches and mudflats

Upland sandpiper	*Bartramia longicauda*		p,b	p,b,(h. 1979),m	meadows and hayfields
Little tern	*Sterna albifrons antillarum*	r,b	r,b	r,b	beaches and bays
Royal tern	*Sterna maxima*		p,b	p,b	spoil banks and sandy islands
Sandwich tern	*Thalasseus sandvicensis acuflavidus*		p,b(h. 1974)	p,b	beaches and spoil banks
Gull-billed tern	*Geochelidon nilotica aranea*		p,b(h. 1975)	p,b	spoil banks, marshes, and bays
Bewick's wren	*Thyromanes bewickii altus*		p,b	p,b	thickets and fencerows
Sedge wren	*Cistothorus platensis stellaris*	p,b,w	p,b,w	p,b,w	*Spartina* marshes and meadows
Golden-crowned kinglet	*Regulus satrapa*	p,w	p,b,w	p,b,w	coniferous woodlands
Eastern loggerhead shrike	*Lanius ludovicianus ludovicianus*		p,b	p,b	hedgerows and edges
Migrant loggerhead shrike	*Lanius ludovicianus migrans*	p,b,w	p,b,w	p,b,w	hedgerows and edges
Nashville warbler	*Vermivora ruficapilla*		p,b	p,v	mixed woods, bogs, and edges
Dickcissel	*Spiza americana*		p,b,m	p,b,m	clover and alfalfa fields
Grasshopper sparrow	*Ammodramus savannarum pratensis*	r,b	r,b	r,b	hayfields and meadows
Henslow's sparrow	*Ammodramus henslowii susurrans*	p,b	p,b	p,b	broomsedge fields
Swamp sparrow	*Melospiza georgiana nigrescens*	p,b,w	p,b,w	p,b,w	tidal marshes and swamps

Reptiles

Common Name	Scientific Name	Distribution DE	Distribution MD	Distribution VA	Habitat
Bog turtle	*Clemmys muhlenbergi*	d	d	d	bogs, swamps, streams
Mountain earth snake	*Virginia valeriae pulchra*		e(+PA,WV)		deciduous forests, fields
Canebrake rattlesnake	*Crotalus horridus* ssp.			p	thickets and swamps

Amphibians

Common Name	Scientific Name	Distribution DE	Distribution MD	Distribution VA	Habitat
Eastern hellbender	*Cryptobranchus a. alleganiensis*		p	p	aquatic; rivers and streams
Eastern tiger salamander	*Ambystoma tigrinum tigrinum*	r	r	r	underground; woods, fields
Pigmy salamander	*Desmognathus wrighti*			p	high spruce-fir forests
Shovelnose salamander	*Leurognathus marmoratus*			p	aquatic; mountain streams
Spotbelly salamander	*Plethodon welleri*			e(+NC,TN)	high spruce forest
White-spotted salamander	*Plethodon punctatus*			e(+WV)	moist, cool forest
Green salamander	*Aneides aeneus*		p	p	cliffs in hardwood forests

Fishes

Common Name	Scientific Name	Distribution DE	Distribution MD	Distribution VA	Habitat
Atlantic sturgeon	*Acipenser oxyrhynchus*	r	r	r	rivers, bay, and ocean
Roanoke bass	*Ambloplites cavifrons*			e(+NC)	clear, warm streams
Blackbanded sunfish	*Enneacanthus chaetodon*	?	r	r	still, acidic freshwater
Ashy darter	*Etheostoma cinereum*			r	clear, warm streams
Finescale saddled darter	*Etheostoma osburni*			e(+WV)	clear, warm streams
Tippecanoe darter	*Etheostoma tippecanoe*			p	clear, warm streams
Duskytail darter	*Etheostoma* sp.			e(+TN)	clear, warm streams
Tangerine darter	*Percina aurantiaca*			r	clear, warm streams
Blotchside darter	*Percina burtoni*			p	clear, warm streams
Northern logperch	*Percina caprodes semifasciata*		d	d (h.1938)	clear, warm streams
Channel darter	*Percina copelandi*			p	clear, warm streams
Longhead darter	*Percina macrocephala*			p	clear, warm streams

Glossary

Acid mine drainage - Acidic run-off from mine tailings and spoils (e.g., iron ore and coal) which pollutes streams and groundwater.

Acid rain - Natural rainfall that contains sulfuric and nitric acids as a result of sulfur dioxide and oxides of nitrogen discharged into the air by power plants, industries, and automobiles.

Adipose fin - The posterior fin of certain fish located between the dorsal fin and the caudal, or tail, fin.

Ambergris - A gray waxy substance, composed of squid beaks and other products of digestion, found in the intestine of sperm whales. Utilized by man as a stabilizer in perfume production.

Anadromous - A fish species that ascends rivers from the sea to spawn in freshwater (e.g., salmon, shad, sturgeon).

Avifauna - The birds of a certain region.

Benthic - Relating to or occurring at the bottom of a body of water; bottom dwelling.

Biogeography - The study of the geographical distribution of plant and animal species.

Biota - The flora and fauna of a region.

Carapace - A bony or chitinous shell covering the dorsal surface of an animal, such as a turtle or crab.

Catadromous - A fish species that lives in freshwater, but migrates to the sea to spawn (e.g., American eel).

Caudal spot - Pigmented marking at the base of the tail, or caudal, fin of some fish species.

Costal shields - The rows of scales on the carapace of a turtle between the vertebral shields (dorsal) and the marginal shields (outermost).

Critical habitat - Habitat designated by the U. S. Fish and Wildlife Service as essential to the survival of an endangered or threatened species.

Detritus - Organic material in the process of disintegration and decay.

Disjunct population - A population that is geographically isolated from a main population of a given species.

Diversity - The absolute number of species present in a locality, region, or the world.

Endemic - A species (or subspecies) that is restricted in its distribution to a particular locality or region.

Equilibrium - The state in which rate of death of organisms in a population equals rate of birth, or rate of extinction of species equals rate of speciation.

Estuarine species - A permanent resident of an estuary (a semienclosed body of brackish water that has a measurable salinity gradient from its freshwater tributaries to its ocean entrance).

Extant - A species (or subspecies) that is currently in existence; the opposite of extinct.

Extinction - The total, irreversible disappearance of a species (or subspecies) from the world.

Extirpation - The disappearance, temporarily or permanently, of a species (or subspecies) from a locality or regon.

Filter feeder - An animal species that filters food items from the water by means of a straining mechanism (e.g., gills or baleen).

Gene pool - The totality of genes of a given population existing at a given time.

Gestation - The period during which mammals carry young in the uterus.

Hacking station - A platform or nest box from which young birds, born in captivity, are released into the wild.

Herpetology - The study of amphibians and reptiles.

Icthyofauna - The fishes of a certain region.

Insectivorous - An animal species that exclusively or predominantly forages on insects (e.g., shrews and certain bats).

Krill - Small species of shrimplike crustaceans found in enormous numbers which serve as the major food source for some species of baleen whales.

Local species - A species limited to a relatively small area in the region(s) where it occurs.

Marginal shields - The outermost row of scales at the edge of the carapace of a turtle.

Migrant - A regular visitor in a region during the migration season(s).

Mixed hardwood forest - A forest consisting of deciduous trees (hardwoods) mixed with conifers (e.g., pine, spruce, hemlock).

Omnivorous - An organism that feeds on both animals and plants.

Pereopods - Leglike thoracic appendages found on crustaceans and certain other arthropods.

Peripheral population - A population at the extreme limit of its range within a certain locality or regon.

Pesticide - A chemical agent used to destroy pests (e.g., weeds and harmful insects). Chlorinated pesticides, including DDT, dieldrin, and endrin, cause eggshell thining in birds and other deleterious effects.

Phylum - A primary taxonomic division of the animal or plant kingdom.

Plankton - The minute animal and plant life that passively floats or weakly swims in a body of water.

Plastron - The ventral part of the shell of certain organisms (e.g., turtles and crabs).

Population, local - The community of potentially interbreeding individuals at a given locality.

Siltation - The process of suspension and deposition of sedimentary material, or silt, in a body of water that often results in the suffocation of benthic organisms.

Spawning - The deposition of many small eggs by certain aquatic animals (e.g., fish and oysters).

Speciation - The splitting of a phyletic line; the process of the multiplication of species.

Spermaceti - An oily substance found in the heads of some toothed whales. Used by man as a high quality oil and opaque wax.

Species - A reproductively isolated aggregate of interbreeding populations.

Subspecies - An assemblage of local populations of a species inhabiting a geographical subdivision of the range of the species and differing taxonomically from other populations of the species.

Taxon (pl. taxa) - A set of species: either a single species or a group of species that together constitute a higher taxonomic unit such as a genus or family.

Transient - a rare or unusual visitor in a region.

Trophic level - The hierarchical stratum in a food chain characterized by organisms that are the same number of steps removed from the primary producers.

Turbidity - Decreased clarity in a body of water as a result of suspension of silt.

Whorl - An arrangement of three or more leaves, sepals, or flowers originating from a single point on a stem.

Selected References

Borror, D. J., and White, R. E., 1970. *A field guide to the insects of America north of Mexico.* Houghton Mifflin Co., Boston. 404 p.

Burt, W. H., and Grossenheider, R. P., 1976. *A field guide to the mammals.* Houghton Mifflin Co., Boston. 289 p.

Coffey, D. J., 1977. *Dolphins, whales, and porpoises: an encyclopedia of sea mammals.* Macmillan Publishing Co., New York. 300 p.

Conant, R., 1975. *A field guide to reptiles and amphibians of eastern and central North America.* Houghton Mifflin Co., Boston. 429 p.

Linzey, D. W. (editor), 1979. *Endangered and threatened plants and animals of Virginia.* Virginia Polytechnic Institute, Blacksburg, Virginia. 665 p.

MacArthur, R. H., and Wilson, E. O., 1967. *The theory of island biogeography.* Princeton University Press, Princeton, New Jersey. 203 p.

Norden, A. W., and Forester, D. C. (editors), 1982 (in press). *Endangered and threatened plants and animals of Maryland.* The Nature Conservancy, Arlington, Virginia.

Parker, W., and Dixon, L., 1980. *Endangered and threatened wildlife of Kentucky, North Carolina, South Carolina and Tennessee.* North Carolina Agric. Extension Service, Raleigh, North Carolina. 122 p.

Peterson, R. T., 1980. *A field guide to the birds of eastern and central North America.* Houghton Mifflin Co., Boston. 384 p.

Ripley, S. D., 1975. *Report on endangered and threatened plant species of the United States.* U. S. Government Printing Office, 94th Congress, House Document No. 94-51.

Robbins, C. S., Bruun, B., and Zim, H. S., 1966. *Birds of North America: a guide to field identification.* Golden Press, New York. 340 p.

Index

Aloe, 7
Amphipod
  Alleghany County cave, 82, 131
  Biggers' cave, 82, 131
  Hay's spring, 82, 86, 131
  James Cave, 82, 131
  Luray Caverns, 83, 131
  Madison Cave, 83, 85, 131
Armadillo, 7
Asphodel, bog, 135
Aster, 133
Auk, great, 4, 8, 40

Bald eagle, 7, 9, 40, 41, 44, 130
Bass, Roanoke, 127, 139
Bat, *see also* Myotis.
  eastern big-eared, 21
  Virginia big-eared, 9, 14, 20, 129
Bear, black, 119
Beaver, 119
Beetle
  American burying, 83, 132
  burying, 83, 132
  ground, 83, 132
  sugar maple longhorn, 83, 132
  tiger, 83, 132
Birch
  gray, 116
  sweet, 115
  Virginia round-leaf, 9, 110, 114, 133
Bishop's weed, mock, 135
Bison, 13, 117
Bitter-cress, Long's, 111, 134
Bobcat, 119
  southern, 116, 119
Boneset, 134
Buckwheat, yellow, 134
Bugbane, Kearney's, 134
Bulrush, 135
Bur-marigold, Maryland, 133
Butterfly, 82, 83, *see also* Fritillary

Chaffseed, 135

Chestnut, American, 5
Chub
  slender, 70, 74, 131
  spotfin, 70, 76, 131
Clam, *see also* Mussel
  Atlantic surf, 88
  hard, 88
  soft-shell, 88
Cliff-green, 135
Clover, Virginia, 135
Coneflower
  purple, 134
  sun-facing, 135
Cottontail rabbit
  eastern, 14, 15
  New England, 119
Cougar
  eastern, 8, 9, 13, 14, 15, 38, 129
  western, 39
Crane, whooping, 4
Curlew, Eskimo, 41
Cypress, bald, 116

Damselfly, 83, 132
Darter
  ashy, 127, 139
  blotchside, 127, 139
  channel, 127, 139
  duskytail, 127, 139
  finescale saddled, 127, 139
  longhead, 127, 139
  Maryland, 7, 9, 70, 80, 131
  sharphead, 71, 131
  snail, 4, 7
  tangerine, 127, 139
  Tippecanoe, 127, 139
Deer, white-tailed, 8, 39
Dickcissel, 121, 137
Dolphin, 25
Dropwort, 135
Duck, Labrador, 5, 40

Eagle, *see* Bald eagle.
Elk, 4, 13, 117
  eastern, 4

INDEX

Falcon, *see* Peregrine falcon.
Fisher, 13, 118, 136
Fox squirrel, *see* Squirrel.
Fritillary, regal, 83, 132

Gallberry, 134
Gentian, 134
  pine-barren, 134
Goldenrod, shale barren, 135
Goshawk, 121
Guyandotte beauty, 135

Hare, snowshoe, 116, 118, 136
Harrier, northern, 121
Hawk, sharp-shinned, 121
Heath-hen, 5, 40
Hellbender, eastern, 124, 138
Holly, long-stalked, 135

Isopod
  Madison Cave, 82, 84, 131
  Rye Cove cave, 82, 131

Kinglet, golden-crowned, 121, 137

Leather flower, 110, 134
  white-haired, 134
Lemming, southern bog, 13, 15, 129
Leopard, snow, 7
Lewis' heart-leaf, 134
Lily, Gray's, 134
Loggerhead shrike
  eastern, 117, 121, 137
  migrant, 121, 137
Logperch
  northern, 127, 139
  Roanoke, 71, 131
Lousewort, furbish, 4

Madtom
  orangefin, 71, 131
  yellowfin, 70, 78, 131
Manatee, 13
Micrantheum, 135
Minnow, *see* Chub.
Mole, southern star-nosed, 119

Molluscs, 7, 82, *see* Snail *and* Mussel.
Moth, clear-wing, 5
Mountain lion, *see* Cougar.
Mussel, 9, 88, 93
  acorn, pearly, 89, 133
  Appalachian monkey-face pearly, 94, 97, 132
  birdwing pearly, 98, 132
  Cumberland monkey-face pearly, 96, 132
  dromedary pearly, 97, 100, 133
  fine-rayed pigtoe pearly, 106, 133
  fine-rayed purple pearly, 89, 133
  freshwater (*Lasmigona holstonia*), 89, 133
  freshwater (*Lastena lata*), 89, 133
  green-blossom pearly, 102, 133
  little-winged pearly, 89, 133
  shiny pigtoe, 108, 133
  tan riffle shell, 104, 133
  Virginia spiny, 89, 133
Myotis
  gray, 9, 14, 15, 16, 129
  Indiana, 9, 14, 18, 129

Nestronia, 135

Orchid, 135
  white-fringed prairie, 135
Osprey, 41, 121
Owl, short-eared, 120, 121
Oyster, Virginia, 88

Parakeet, Carolina, 4, 5, 40
Parsley, 134
Pelican, eastern brown, 9, 41, 42, 130

Peregrine falcon, 7, 9
  American, 40, 46, 49, 120, 130
  Arctic, 41, 47, 48, 129
Periwinkle plant, Madagascar, 7
Peters Mountain mellow, 134
Phlox, swordleaf, 135
Pigeon, passenger, 4, 5, 40, 116

INDEX

Pimpernel, mountain, 110, 135
Piratebush, 134
Planarian
   Biggers' groundwater, 82
   Holsinger's groundwater, 82
   Rockbridge County groundwater, 82
Plover
   piping, 121, 136
   Wilson's, 116, 121, 136
Pogonia
   small whorled, 110, 112, 134
   whorled, 113
Porcupine, 118, 119, 136
Porpoise, 25
Pupfish, Tecopa, 4, 8

Quillwort, 134

Rabbit, *see also* Cottontail rabbit, Hare.
   marsh, 119
Ragwort, pussytoes, 110, 135
Rat
   black, 8
   Norway, 8
Rattlesnake
   canebrake, 116, 122, 138
Rattlesnake root, 135
Reed, sand, 134
Rush
   Knieskern's beaked, 135
   New Jersey, 134

Salamander, 56, 57, 124, 125, *see also* Hellbender.
   eastern tiger, 124, 138
   green, 124, 138
   Jefferson, 116, 125
   Peaks of Otter, 57, 124
   pigmy, 125, 138
   Shenandoah, 57, 124
   shovelnose, 125, 138
   spotbelly, 125, 138
   Virginia seal, 57
   white-spotted, 125, 138
Sandpiper, upland, 121, 137
Saxifrage
   Carey, 135
   Carolina, 135

Sea cow, Steller's, 8
Sedge, 134
Sensitive joint-vetch, 133
Shad
   American, 6, 126
   Hickory, 126
Shiner, roughhead, 71
Shrew, 15
   Dismal Swamp, 13, 15, 129
   long-tailed, 119
   northern water, 14, 129
   pygmy, 14, 15, 129
   swamp short-tailed, 13, 15, 129
Shrike, *see* Loggerhead shrike.
Skink, northern coal, 123
Snail
   Socorro, 8
   spiny river, 89, 132
   Virginia fringed mountain, 9, 89, 90, 132
Snake, *see also* Rattlesnake.
   glossy crawfish, 123
   mountain earth, 122, 138
   northern pine, 123
   rainbow, 123
   red-bellied water, 123
   southeastern crown, 123
Sparrow
   Bachman's, 116, 120
   grasshopper, 116, 121, 137
   Henslow's, 121, 137
   swamp, 121, 137
Squirrel
   Delmarva Peninsula fox, 6, 9, 13, 14, 15, 22, 129
   gray, 23
   northern flying, 14, 118, 129
Stargrass, Long's, 5, 111
Stonecrop, 135
Sturgeon
   Atlantic, 127, 139
   shortnose, 6, 9, 71, 72, 127, 131
Sucker
   harelip, 5, 70
   rustyside, 71
Sunfish, blackbanded, 127, 139
Swamp pink, 111, 134

Tern
   gull-billed, 121, 137
   little, 120, 137

roseate, 6, 116, 120
royal, 120, 137
sandwich, 120, 137
Terrapin, *see also* Turtle.
 northern diamondback, 122
Toad, eastern narrow-mouth, 125
Trout-perch, 117
Turtle, *see also* Terrapin.
 bog, 116, 117, 122, 138
 green, 56, 58, 60, 130
 hawksbill, 56, 57, 58, 59, 61, 62, 130
 Kemp's ridley, 56, 58, 66, 130
 leatherback, 56, 58, 59, 65, 68, 130
 loggerhead, 56, 58, 59, 64, 130
 sea, 9, 56, 59

Warbler
 Bachman's, 7, 40, 41, 52, 130
 Kirtland's, 9, 41, 54, 120, 130
 Nashville, 121, 137
Water-hyssop, 5, 111, 133
Weasel, least, 119
Whale, 9, 13, 14, 15
 black right, 25, 33, 37, 129
 blue, 15, 25, 28, 31, 33, 129
 bowhead, 31
 fin, 25, 29, 30, 33, 129
 humpback, 25, 33, 34, 129
 sei, 25, 32, 129
 sperm, 15, 25, 26, 129
Wolf's milk spurge, 134
Wren
 Bewick's, 121, 137
 sedge, 116, 121, 137
Wolf, gray, 8
Woodpecker
 ivory-billed, 6
 red-cockaded, 9, 40, 41, 50, 130

Picture Credits

Front Cover: Bald eagle. Photo by Buck Miller, Raptor Information Center, National Wildlife Federation

Back Cover: Small whorled pogonia, an endangered plant in the Chesapeake Bay region. Photo by Dick Dyer

Burch, P. R., Drawing, 92
Clark, William S., Raptor Information Center, National Wildlife Federation, 44
Clarke, Herbert, USFWS, 117 (Eastern loggerhead shrike)
Couch, Jim, Georgia Department of Natural Resources, 72
Curtsinger, William R., 26, 30, 34
Dittrick, Robert, USFWS, 60
Dixon, Laura, USFWS, 52, 78
Du Rant, William, *South Carolina Wildlife Magazine*, 38, 46
Etnier, David A., USFWS, 76
Ford, Winifred, USFWS, 117 (Bog turtle)
Hagan, Pat, USFWS, 64
Harris, John L., USFWS, 74
Jones, Wes, Michigan Department of Natural Resources, 54
Julian, William H., USFWS, 22, 50
MacGregor, John, 20
Meyer, F. G., USFWS, 114
Parnell, James F., 42
Porter, Stuart, USFWS, 66
Pritchard, Peter C. H., 62, 68
Raptor Information Center, National Wildlife Federation, Map, 44
Schwartz, F. J., 1962. Drawing, *Turtles of Maryland.* Second edition, 58
Smith, Michael L., USFWS, 48
Spreitzer, A. E., 94, 96, 98, 100, 102, 104, 106, 108
Stuckey, I. M., USFWS, 112
Tuttle, Merlin D., Milwaukee Public Museum, 16, 18
U. S. Department of Commerce (NOAA), Painting, 24, 28, 32, 36
White, Christopher P., 84, 86, 90
Williams, James, USFWS, 80